OUT
IN THE
DARK

POETRY
OF THE FIRST WORLD WAR
IN CONTEXT AND WITH BASIC NOTES

DAVID ROBERTS

SAXON BOOKS

ISBN 0 9528969 1 5

Saxon Books   221 London Road   Burgess Hill   West Sussex   RH15 9RN
Great Britain
Phone/fax 01444 23 23 56

First published 1998

The acknowledgements constitute an extension of this copyright page.

Printed and bound in Great Britain by The Ipswich Book Company Limited, Ipswich.

CONTENTS

Titles of poems are in italics

Acknowledgements

I am grateful to all who have helped me in the production of this book, especially John Bedford who proof read it. I am grateful, too, to all who have granted me permission to use copyright material.

DR

Poetry and Prose

For the Fallen by Lawrence Binyon, by permission of The Society of Authors, on behalf of the Lawrence Binyon Estate; *Thiepval Wood* by Edmund Blunden by permission of the Peters Fraser and Dunlop Group Ltd on behalf of the estate of Edmund Blunden; *Wake Up England* by Robert Bridges, by permission of Lord Bridges; Vera Brittain's *To My Brother* and *Hospital Sanctuary*, Erskine Macdonald, 1918, and The Imperial War Museum, London, 1995, by Permission of her literary executors, Paul Berry and Mark Bostridge; the extracts from Vera Brittain's *Testament of Youth*, by permission of her literary executors, Paul Berry and Mark Bostridge and Victor Gollancz Ltd; *Praematuri* by Margaret Postgate Cole by permission of HJD Cole; *Pluck* by Eva Dobell by permission of Stephen Dobell; *Now That You Too* by Eleanor Farjeon from *First and Second Love*, published by Oxford, by permission of David Higham Associates; *Picardy* by John Galsworthy by permission of the Galsworthy Estate; Rudyard Kipling's *A Dead Statesman, For All We Have And Are,* extract from *Hymn Before Action,* extract from *A Song of the English, A song of the White Men, Common Form* – by permission of A P Watt Ltd on behalf of The National Trust; Wilfred Owen's *To a Comrade in Flanders, An Imperial Elegy, 1914,* and a verse from *The Ballad of Purchase Money,* from *The Complete Poems of Wilfred Owen,* edited by Jon Stallworthy, published by Chatto and Windus,1983, by permission of the estate of Wilfred Owen and Chatto and Windus; extracts from the letters of Wilfred Owen from *Collected Letters of Wilfred Owen,* edited by Harold Owen and John Bell, Oxford University Press © 1967, reprinted by permission of Oxford University Press; the poems of Siegfried Sassoon from *Collected Poems of Siegfried Sassoon,* © 1918,1920, by E P Dutton, © 1936, 1946, 1947, 1948 by Siegfried Sassoon, by permission of George Sassoon and Viking Penguin, a division of Penguin Books USA Inc.

Illustrations

Rachel Fuller pages 72, 73; Hulton Getty © 1998 23, 53 and cover; The Trustees of the Imperial War Museum, London 22, 35, 80, 90, 127, 134, 166; Peace Pledge Union 57; Saxon Picture Library 65, 88a, 91, 108, 118, 132, 138, 176; Saxon Picture Library and the estate of Gavin Roberts © 1988 and 1998: 88b, 142, 160, 171.

INTRODUCTION

The First World War and the Poets

One of the greatest tragedies the world has ever experienced was the First World War. With absolute determination, nations dedicated every ounce of human talent, energy and resources to the destruction of human life. Countless millions were killed; countless millions were disabled by hideous wounds, mental breakdown, bereavement. Life was worsened throughout Europe and the effects were long-lasting.

In the history of mankind war has been a rare and quite abnormal state of affairs, and when wars broke out in earlier centuries most were confined to quite small numbers of participants fighting for a few hours or days with simple weapons.

The First World War announced the century of war. It was to be a century in which whole nations would suffer and support war and the destructive power developed by scientists would create death, misery and brutalisation, on a new and quite astonishing scale. The human race had moved into the era of scientific savagery.

The poets played their part in this war as promoters of it, onlookers, soldiers and victims. What sets them apart is that the poets were those most gifted to express the experience of those shocking years. And their work includes some of the greatest poems in the English language.

1

BRITAIN DREAMS OF WAR

When Great Britain declared war on Germany on the 4th of August 1914 a wave of enthusiasm spread over the country. Almost everyone felt that the war was right and every fit young man should fight for his country and destroy the German army. Every national newspaper proclaimed the need to take up arms against the wicked enemy.

A few days earlier most people in Britain had been firmly *against* declaring war. But then a huge German army marched into Belgium on its way to attack France. The injustice of this unprovoked attack on a small nation filled the British people with anger – and perhaps a little fear too.

The anger was understandable, but why was it so powerful that the British people, almost overnight, decided to go beyond anger and risk everything in a commitment to all-out war against Germany?

THE LONG PREPARATION FOR WAR

At the start of the twentieth century Britain was a remarkable country. It controlled the largest empire the world has ever seen - about a quarter of the earth. It had very successful industries – but was being overtaken by America and Germany. Its farming, though part of the wonderful English countryside so often celebrated by poets, was failing badly. It produced less than half of the food needed to feed the nation.

The British traded with, and tried to live in peace with, neighbouring European countries – while controlling the 400 million people in overseas territories by military force. The military control was, in fact, quite weak, and only succeeded because, for the most part, the inhabitants of British colonies had no modern weapons. The army based in Britain was small and quite inadequate for fighting a war in Europe. The alternative to armies is friendship. For this reason the British tried to make friendly agreements with all large countries (including Russia, Japan, and France) that could be a danger to Britain and her colonies.

Many people realised the military weakness of Britain and knew Germany was developing and training a massive army and navy. Some of them started to try to persuade the politicians and people of Britain of the need to improve and increase British military strength.

This organised campaign of persuasion was led by old soldiers (like Earl Roberts), writers (including James Garvin, William Le Queux, GA Henty, Erskine Caldwell, Henry Newbolt and Rudyard Kipling), and the newspaper proprietor Alfred Harmsworth (Lord Northcliffe) who used his newspapers to encourage a fear of Germany, and his wealth to pay writers to write popular fiction in which Germany was shown as the enemy of Britain. *The Invasion*, published in 1910, which Harmsworth asked Le Queux to write, sold over a million copies. As one result of their campaigns, enormous new battleships (the Dreadnoughts) were built at great expense, and the territorial army was set up.

H G Wells complained bitterly of the effects of using money for war preparations.

> Mankind, we saw too late, had been guilty of an incalculable folly in permitting men to make a profit out of the dreadful preparations for war. But the evil was started; the German imagination was captured and enslaved. On every other European country that valued its integrity was thrust the overwhelming necessity to arm and drill . . . Money was withdrawn from education, from social progress, from every kind of human happiness; life was drilled and darkened.

In spite of the anti-German stories that had been put about for many years it is possible that before the 4th of August 1914 most people in Britain doubted that Germany was a real threat, and many admired Germany's industrial achievement, music and literature. Then, Germany's brutal march into Belgium turned their worst fears to reality.

Education for militarism before the First World War

It was from the public schools that almost all the officers of the British army were chosen. These schools prepared boys to think of fighting as wonderful and glorious, and to believe that the greatest thing any man could do was to die for his country. Such an education provided thousands of war-ready young men when Lord Kitchener called them to fight for King and Country.

Henry Newbolt, who went on to promote ideas of warrior heroism through his poetry, and as a propagandist at the Ministry of Information, certainly loved the idea of fighting which he picked up in his days at school. In his prep school in Caistor, Lincolnshire, his headmaster would interrupt stories of the heroes of Ancient Greece to give the class up to the minute news of real life "heroic deeds" of the British army in Africa.

"The young of my generation," he later wrote, "had neither cruel experience nor dark apprehension to weaken them. We expected fighting and we prepared for it: but we felt as mighty as the heroes and heroines in the great sagas and trusted ourselves to Destiny with incredible confidence."

Before the war, schools loved to teach, and the general public loved to read "fighting verse." This verse encouraged boys to become soldier heroes willing to die for their country - which really meant fighting to capture weaker countries or keep them under British control.

Admirals All was the title poem from Newbolt's best-selling collection of poetry and celebrated the heroes of Britain's sea battles. It was published seventeen years before the First World War, and sold twenty-one thousand copies in its first year. In it, *Vitai Lampada (The Torch of Life)* famously linked the ideas of war and duty with sportsmanship.

In *Clifton Chapel* Newbolt linked ideas of heroic death with God, school, brotherhood and loving the game (of war) "beyond the prize." Clifton Chapel, and Clifton College at which Newbolt was a student, along with Field Marshal Sir Douglas Haig, certainly convinced students that it was great to be a soldier for three thousand of Clifton College's former students fought in the war.

At the start of the conflict Newbolt put together a collection of his most warlike verse. Within a short space of time it had sold 70,000 copies.

Rudyard Kipling, one of the most popular writers of his day, also celebrated England's soldiers, and linked God with England's conquests (*A Song of the English* and *Hymn Before Action*). In *A Song of the White Men* he associated "the white men" with war, conquest and purification

How young public schoolboys accepted the idea of being a soldier and fighting is seen in Charles Sorley's poems, *A Call to Action*, and *The Massacre,* which he wrote when he was seventeen. (See pages 47 and 48.)

VITAI LAMPADA [1]

There's a breathless hush in the Close tonight –
Ten to make and the match to win –
A bumping pitch and a blinding light,
An hour to play and the last man in.
And it's not for the sake of a ribboned coat,
Or the selfish hope of a season's fame,
But his Captain's hand on his shoulder smote –
"Play up! play up! and play the game!"

The sand of the desert is sodden red, –
Red with the wreck of a square [2] that broke; –
The Gatling's [3] jammed and the Colonel dead,
And the regiment blind with dust and smoke.
The river of death has brimmed his banks,
And England's far, and Honour a name,
But the voice of a schoolboy rallies the ranks:
"Play up! play up! and play the game!"

This is the word that year by year,
While in her place the School is set,
Every one of her sons must hear,
And none that hears it dare forget.
This they all with a joyful mind
Bear through life like a torch in flame,
And falling fling to the host behind –
"Play up! play up! and play the game!"

Henry Newbolt, June, 1892

1 *Vitai Lampada* - the torch of life, a flaming torch symbolising life, and here seen as a baton
passed to succeeding generations as if to runners in a relay race   2 military formation   3 early,
hand-cranked machine gun

From ADMIRALS ALL

Admirals all, they said their say
(The echoes are ringing still),
Admirals all, they went their way
To the haven under the hill.
But they left us a kingdom none can take,
The realm of the circling sea,
To be ruled by the rightful sons of Blake
And the Rodneys[1] yet to be.

Admirals all, for England's sake,
Honour be yours and fame!
And honour, as long as waves shall break,
To Nelson's[2] peerless[3] name!

Henry Newbolt, November, 1892

1 Baron George Rodney,1719-1792. In 1759 commander of the ships which destroyed at Le Havre
a French fleet that was preparing to invade England. Following naval battles with the Spanish and
French he captured the Leeward Islands and Dutch islands in the West Indies   2 Viscount Horatio
Nelson, 1758-1805. British naval hero who beat the French at the Battles of the Nile and Trafalgar
3 without equal, greatest

CLIFTON[1] CHAPEL

This is the Chapel: here, my son,
Your father thought the thoughts of youth,
And heard the words that one by one
The touch of Life has turned to truth.
Here in a day that is not far
You too may speak with noble ghosts
Of manhood and the vows of war
You made before the Lord of Hosts.[2]

To set the cause above renown,
To love the game beyond the prize,
To honour, while you strike him down,
The foe that comes with fearless eyes;
To count the life of battle good,
And dear the land that gave you birth,
And dearer yet the brotherhood
That binds the brave of all the earth.

My son, the oath[3] is yours: the end
Is His, Who built the world of strife,
Who gave His children Pain for friend,
And Death for surest hope of life.
Today and here the fight's begun,
Of the great fellowship[4] you're free;
Henceforth the School and you are one,
And what You are, the race shall be.

God send you fortune: yet be sure,
Among the lights that gleam and pass,
You'll live to follow none more pure
Than that which glows on yonder brass:[5]
"Qui procul hinc," the legend's writ, –
The frontier-grave is far away –
"Qui ante diem periit:
Sed miles, sed pro patria."[6]

Henry Newbolt

1 a public school in Bristol   2 *Lord of Hosts* - God   3 solemn promise   4 association of friends
5 *Yonder brass* was one of Newbolts's poetic inventions. No such brass or inscription exists in
Clifton Chapel. 6 *Qui procul hinc, qui ante diem periit: sed miles, sed pro patria.* – He who died
so far from home, died before his time: but he was a soldier, and it was for his country he died.

FAREWELL

Mother, with unbowed head
Hear thou across the sea
The farewell of the dead,
The dead who died for thee.
Greet them again with tender words and grave,
For, saving thee, themselves they could not save.

To keep the house unharmed
Their fathers built so fair,
Deeming[1] endurance armed[2]
Better than brute despair,[3]
They found the secret of the word that saith,
"Service is sweet, for all true life is death."

So greet thou well[4] thy dead
Across the homeless sea,
And be thou comforted
Because they died for thee.
Far off they served, but now their deed is done
For evermore their life and thine are one.

Henry Newbolt, 18 January, 1910
Reprinted in *The Times,* 23 September, 1914.

1 believing   2 *endurance armed* - being equipped with weapons and determined to fight and
survive 3 *brute despair* - giving up like an animal   4 *greet thou well* - welcome home your dead
sons

From HYMN BEFORE ACTION

The earth is full of anger,
The seas are dark with wrath,
The Nations in their harness[1]
Go up against our path:[2]
Ere yet we loose the legions –[3]
Ere yet we draw the blade,
Jehovah of the Thunders,
Lord God of Battles, aid!

High lust and froward bearing,[4]
Proud heart, rebellious brow –
Deaf ear and soul uncaring,

We seek Thy mercy now!
The sinner that forswore[5] Thee,
The fool that passed Thee by,
Our times are known before Thee –
Lord, grant us strength to die!

Rudyard Kipling, 1896

1 *in their harness* - prepared for war   2 *Go up against our path* - gathering on our border   3 *loose
the legions* - send armies into battle   4 *High lust and froward bearing* - (with) noble energy and
obstinacy   5 rejected, gave up belief

A SONG OF THE WHITE MEN

Now, this is the cup the White Men drink[1]
When they go to right a wrong,
And that is the cup of the old world's hate –
Cruel and strained and strong.
We have drunk that cup – and a bitter, bitter cup –
And tossed the dregs away.
But well for the world when the White Men drink
To the dawn of the White Man's day![2]

Now, this is the road that the White Men tread
When they go to clean a land –[3]
Iron underfoot[4] and levin[5] overhead
And the deep on either hand.
We have trod that road – and a wet and windy road –
Our chosen star for guide.
Oh, well for the world when the White Men tread
Their highway side by side!

Now, this is the faith that the White Men hold
When they build their homes afar –
"Freedom for ourselves and freedom for our sons
And, failing[6] freedom, War."
We have proved our faith – bear witness[7] to our faith,
Dear souls of freemen[8] slain!
Oh, well for the world when the White Men join
To prove their faith again!

Rudyard Kipling, 1899

1 these are the fortunes experienced   2 *the dawn of the White Man's day* - the start of white races
ruling over other races   3 *clean a land* - rid a land of bad things   4 *iron under foot* etc - suggests
the idea of difficulties everywhere   5 lightning   6 lacking, if we don't have   7 *bear witness* -
prove, show by our actions   8 the white races

White men with natives in Africa in the days of the British Empire.

From A SONG OF THE ENGLISH

Fair is our lot –[1] O goodly is our heritage![2]
(Humble ye, my people, and be fearful in your mirth!)
For the lord our God Most High
He hath made the deep as dry,[3]
He hath smote[4] for us a pathway to the ends of all the Earth!

Rudyard Kipling, 1893
Reprinted in *The Morning Post*, 10 August, 1914.

1 *Fair is our lot* - we are fortunate people   2 lands, property and other things left to us by those who lived before us   3 *made the deep as dry* - made deep waters into dry land, meaning cleared away all obstacles   4 cut

2

THE WAR BEGINS

The first time the English Cabinet discussed the possibility of actually declaring war on Germany was the 24th of July 1914, only eleven days before the decision was taken. The main concerns of the British Government at that time were increasing strikes and threats of strikes in British industry and trouble in Ireland.

In 1914, when the whole of Ireland was part of Great Britain, Government ministers were greatly worried by the threat of civil war in the north of Ireland. On the 24th of July the Prime Minister, Henry Asquith, believed that Great Britain would not need to take part in a war with Germany. For the next seven days, whilst some people felt Germany's threats to enter Belgium should be met by the British army most businessmen and most of the ruling Liberal Party were completely against fighting a war with Germany.

By the 2nd of August Asquith thought that Britain *might* need to fight and ordered that the army should prepare for action. As the German army assembled on Belgium's border more and more newspapers said Britain must fight. Edward Grey, the British Foreign Secretary, issued an ultimatum to Germany stating that if Germany did not agree to keep out of Belgium then Britain would declare war. The deadline was set for 11pm British Summer Time on the 4th of August. The crowds that swarmed around the centre of London that Bank Holiday weekend shouted for war, believing that in a few weeks or months the British army would smash the German army and teach the Germans a lesson.

When Germany failed to promise to keep out of Belgium, Great Britain declared war. Enormous crowds in Trafalgar Square and outside Buckingham Palace chanted and cheered at the thought of beating the Germans. – But there were a few people who were against the war.

A REVERSAL OF VALUES

On the 13th of August, Bertrand Russell (who was later dismissed from his post at Cambridge University and sent to prison for his views about the war) wrote in *Nation*,

A month ago Europe was a peaceful comity of nations; if an Englishman killed a German, he was hanged. Now if an Englishman kills a German, or if a German kills an Englishman, he is a patriot, who has deserved well of his country. We scan the newspapers with greedy eyes for news of slaughter, and rejoice when we read of innocent young men, blindly obedient to the word of command, mown down in thousands by the machine-guns of Liège.

Those who saw the London crowds, during the nights leading up to the Declaration of War saw a whole population, hitherto peaceable and humane, precipitated in a few days down the steep slope to primitive barbarism, letting loose, in a moment, the instincts of hatred and blood lust against which the whole fabric of society has been raised . . .

And all this madness, all this rage, all this flaming death of our civilisation and our hopes, has been brought about because a set of official gentlemen, living luxurious lives, mostly stupid, and all without imagination or heart, have chosen that it should occur rather than that any one of them should suffer some infinitesimal rebuff to his country's pride.

RESPONSE OF POETS TO THE DECLARATION OF WAR

When war was declared a number of poets lacked enthusiasm for it, including Wilfred Owen, Isaac Rosenberg, Edward Thomas, Rupert Brooke and, especially, Charles Sorley. (Details of their responses are to be found in sections devoted to them. Brooke's early doubts disappeared for a time and he wrote his pro-war *1914* sonnets.) But they were exceptional. The majority of poets and versifiers took up their pens to support the war and the newspapers quickly printed their fighting verse.

The first in print was William Watson (who was later awarded a knighthood for his "poetic" support.) Others quickly followed.

TO THE TROUBLER OF THE WORLD

At last we know you, War-lord. You, that flung
The gauntlet down,[1] fling down the mask you wore,
Publish your heart,[2] and let its pent[3] hate pour,
You that had God for ever on your tongue.
We are old in war, and if in guile[4] we are young,
Young also is the spirit that evermore
Burns in our bosom[5] ev'n as heretofore,[6]
Nor are these thews unbraced, these nerves unstrung.[7]

We do not with God's name make wanton play;[8]
We are not on such easy terms with Heaven;
But in Earth's hearing we can verily[9] say,
"Our hands are pure; for peace, for peace we have striven."[10]
And not by Earth shall he be soon forgiven
Who lit the fire accurst[11] that flames today.

William Watson,
The Times, 6 August, 1914

1 *flung the gauntlet down* - threw down the challenge   2 *Publish your heart* - tell the truth
3 repressed, bottled up   4 deceit, trickery 5 *Burns in our bosom* - longs   6 *as heretofore* - as it
used to do   7 *Nor are thews unbraced, nerves unstrung* - we are prepared   8 *make wanton play* -
talk lightly   9 truly   10 worked   11 *Who lit the fire accurst* - he who started this trouble

THE TRIUMPH OF "CULTURE"

A *Punch* magazine cartoon of 26th August 1914. – Many Germans were influenced by one of their
leading historians and political thinkers, Heinrich von Treitschke. He taught that war was noble, and
that in war a man, "for his country's sake must crush his natural feelings of humanity" and murder is
"one of the glories of war." See *Treitschke and the Great War* by Joseph McCabe, T Fisher Unwin,
November 1914.

WAKE UP, ENGLAND

Thou careless,[1] awake!
Thou peace-maker, fight!
Stand, England,[2] for honour,
And God guard the Right!

Thy mirth lay aside,
Thy cavil[3] and play:
The foe is upon thee,
And grave is the day.

The monarch Ambition
Hath harnessed his slaves;[4]
But the folk of the Ocean[5]
Are free as the waves.

For Peace thou art armed
Thy Freedom to hold:
Thy Courage as iron,
Thy Good-faith as gold.

Through Fire, Air, and Water
Thy trial must be:
But they that love life best
Die gladly for thee.

The Love of their mothers
Is strong to command:
The fame of their fathers
Is might to their hand.

Much suffering shall cleanse thee:[6]
But thou through the flood
Shalt win to Salvation,
To Beauty through blood.[7]

Up, careless, awake!
Ye peacemakers, Fight!
ENGLAND STANDS FOR HONOUR.
GOD DEFEND THE RIGHT!

Robert Bridges,
The Times, 8 August, 1914

1 *Thou careless* - apathetic, indifferent people   2 *Stand, England* - let England do the right thing
3 silly objections   4 *monarch Ambition hath harnessed his slaves* - the ambitious German leader
(the Kaiser) has advanced his armies (slaves)   5 *folk of the Ocean* - the seafaring British
6 *cleanse thee* - make you better   7 *through blood* - by shedding blood in battle

VERITAS VICTRIX[1]

The Mill of Lies[2] is loud,
Whose overseer, Germania's Over-lord,
Hath overmuch adored
The Over-sword,[3]
And shall be overthrown, with the overproud.

Praised be the overwatching Heavens, that though
Falsehood her blare of brass may pitch yet higher,[4]
Truth hath her trumpets[5] also, and these of gold,
And she can blow
Longer than any liar,
Fronting the sun, high on her mountains old.

William Watson, *The Times*, 10 September, 1914

1 *Veritas Victrix* - truth victorious, good will win   2 *Mill of Lies* - Germany is here accused of producing a great number of lies   3 *Over-sword* - use of warfare   4 *Falsehood her blare of brass may pitch yet higher* - worse lies are to come   5 *Truth hath her trumpets* - truth (honesty and decency) has her supporters (Britain)

The Germans were portrayed to the Americans as brutal animals. This is how the Americans showed Germany in a recruiting poster of 1917.

Other poets who supported the war at the start – and some throughout – included Siegfried Sassoon, Thomas Hardy, Rudyard Kipling, and Julian Grenfell.

Prime Minister says the war is a great duty

On 7th August, 1914, (three days after Britain joined the war) Henry Asquith, the Prime Minister, said in Parliament to loud cheers:

> I do not think any nation ever entered into a great conflict – and this is one of the greatest that history will ever know – with a clearer conscience or stronger conviction that it is fighting not for aggression, not for the maintenance of its own selfish ends, but in defence of principles, the maintenance of which is vital to the civilisation of the world.

> We have a great duty to perform; we have a great truth to fulfil; and I am confident Parliament and the country will enable us to do it.

So many men wanted to join the army to fight the Germans that, at first, recruiting offices couldn't cope with the rush.

HOW PUBLIC SUPPORT WAS ENCOURAGED

Enthusiasm and patriotism were encouraged by newspapers, posters,
poetry, speeches and music hall songs proclaiming the need to fight.
Soon there was a flood of young men besieging the recruiting of-
fices in an effort to join the army.

A MUSIC HALL SONG

. . .Now your country calls you
To play your part in war
And no matter what befalls you
We shall love you all the more.

So come and join the forces
As your fathers did before.
Oh we don't want to lose you
But we think you ought to go
For your king and your country
Both need you so.

We shall want you and miss you
But with all our might and main[1]
We shall cheer you
Thank you, kiss you
When you come back again.

1 *might and main* - strength

Lord Kitchener was appointed Minister for War. He was put in charge
of recruiting the large army needed to fight the war. He asked the coun-
try to give him 100,000 volunteers. His advertisements billed the con-
flict as "the greatest war in the history of the world."

Young people love to indulge in dangerous and life-risking activities,
so it was easy for the government to channel these natural desires into
fighting for England. The call to fight for England also gave thousands
of aimless young men, who had no idea what they wanted to do with
their lives, a real purpose.

Those who first rushed to join wondered if they would be in time.
Everyone was sure of an easy victory. The newspapers encouraged re-
cruiting with the confident prediction that it would "all be over
by Christmas."

Within about eighteen months Kitchener had not 100,000 volunteers,
but two million. Wars run, not on reason, but on adrenalin, base

emotion, hype, and herd instinct. Once a war is started, a kind of madness takes over which is very hard to stop.

Two soldiers explain why they joined the army

> We had been brought up to believe that Britain was the best country in the world and we wanted to defend her. The history taught us at school showed that we were better than other people (didn't we always win the last war?) and now all the news was that Germany was the aggressor and we wanted to show the Germans what we could do.

> Private George Morgan,
> 16th Battalion, West Yorkshire Regiment

> The romance of it . . .   the mystery and uncertainty of it . . . the glowing enthusiasm and lofty idealism of it: of our own free will we were embarked on this glorious enterprise, ready to endure any hardship and make any sacrifice, inspired by a patriotism newly awakened by the challenge to our country's honour.

> Private W T Colyer, First Battalion, Artist's Rifles

Herbert Read's motivation and unrealistic view of war

Herbert Read became a distinguished soldier, academic, critic and poet. He wrote:

> It must be remembered that in 1914 our conception of war was completely unreal. We had vague childish memories of the Boer War, and from these and a general diffusion of Kiplingesque sentiments, we managed to infuse into war a decided element of adventurous romance. War still appealed to the imagination.

> The war meant a decision: a crystalisation of vague projects: an immediate acceptance of the challenge of life. I did not hesitate.

He was commissioned in the Yorkshire Regiment (the Green Howards) in January 1915.

HAPPY IS ENGLAND NOW

There is not anything more wonderful
Than a great people moving towards the deep
Of an unguessed and unfeared future; nor
Is aught[1] so dear of all held dear before
As the new passion stirring in their veins
When the destroying Dragon[2] wakes from sleep.

Happy is England now, as never yet!
And though the sorrows of the slow days fret
Her faithfullest children,[3] grief itself is proud.
Ev'n the warm beauty of this spring and summer
That turns to bitterness turns then to gladness
Since for this England the beloved ones died.

Happy is England in the brave that die
For wrongs not hers and wrongs so sternly hers;
Happy in those that give, give, and endure
The pain that never the new years may cure;
Happy in all her dark woods, green fields, towns,
Her hills and rivers and her chafing sea.

Whate'er was dear before is dearer now.
There's not a bird singing upon his bough
But sings the sweeter in our English ears:
There's not a nobleness of heart, hand, brain,
But shines the purer; happiest is England now
In those that fight, and watch with pride and tears.

John Freeman, 1914

1 anything   2 *destroying Dragon* - Germany   3 *faithfullest children* - the soldier, their parents
and supporters

HAPPY FOR SOME

When poets wrote about England in war-time poetry they always
depicted the countryside. With day after day of blue skies and wonder-
ful summer sunshine, in the golden summer of 1914, the English land-
scape was seen and enjoyed at its best. For poets with minds filled with
such images it was easy to think of England as an ideal and idyllic coun-
try, forget the shortcomings, and that the countryside was not the envi-
ronment best known to most Englishmen.

These were familiar with mills, mines, and factories, industrial towns,
big cities and overcrowded houses lacking basic amenities. (Bathrooms
were almost unheard of in working class homes, and thousands of homes
lacked their own water supply.)

The "land of the free" in 1914 had moved towards democracy, but no
woman had the vote, and, of the men, only those who were house own-
ers. In all, out of 25 million adults, only 8 million men had the vote.

For the working class (about 17 million workers) hours were often long,
wages poor, and conditions harsh. Improvements were gradually taking

place, though. The Shop Hours Act, for example, guaranteed shop workers a minimum of half a day's holiday each week.

From the start of the twentieth century unemployment had been growing in Britain. Widescale hardship was so apparent that charities were set up by the Lord Mayor of London and the Queen "to alleviate the suffering of the poor, starving unemployed." On 1st January 1908 official statistics put the number of paupers in England and Wales at 928,671.

THE SHOCK OF EVENTS IN BELGIUM

The Belgians courageously did all they could to hinder the German advance. Within a few weeks they had torn up 2000 miles of railway track. The Germans brought in 26,000 construction workers to carry out repairs.

But the actions of the Belgians enraged the Germans and they soon carried out reprisals. They burnt homes, looted and destroyed factories, shot civilians (men, women, and children) and carried away 700,000 men to work as slave labourers in Germany.

British newspapers reported fully the plight of the Belgian people, but, as if the truth were not bad enough, they added numerous stories of atrocities which the Germans were supposed to have carried out – such as the spearing of babies, the cutting off of a woman's breasts, and children's hands.

It is no exaggeration to say that the invasion of Belgium shocked the nation and turned against the German people most of those who considered themselves to be pacifists, and those who desired friendship with them. The German threat was real, horrific, and very close to England.

WRITERS ENLISTED IN THE SECRET WAR PROPAGANDA BUREAU

Clearly, writers in the same frame of mind as Rudyard Kipling and Robert Bridges needed little encouragement to write supporting the war effort. However, the Government did not leave the matter to chance. At the end of August Sir Edward Grey and Lloyd George decided to set up a department of propaganda, The Secret War Propaganda Bureau. This was put in the hands of Charles Masterman, a member of the Cabinet.

One of his first ideas was to encourage sympathetic, famous, and influential writers to use their pens in support of the war effort and in particular to spread the "British viewpoint" in America where there was little understanding of the British Government's actions.

He called a meeting of "well-known men of letters" at Wellington House on 2nd September 1914. Those present included Thomas Hardy (then 74), H G Wells, Arnold Bennett, John Galsworthy, John Masefield, Robert Bridges (the Poet Laureate), Conan Doyle, Owen Seaman (Editor of Punch), J M Barrie, G K Chesterton, Israel Zangwill, G M Trevelyan and Gilbert Murray. Rudyard Kipling, unable to attend, sent a message of support. Laurence Binyon was soon to be associated with the group.

Inspired by the meeting, many of those present rapidly set to work to write the kind of thing the government wanted. Hardy's poem, *Men Who March Away,* was quickly taken up by the British and American press: published in *The Times Literary Supplement*, on 10th September, and *The New York Times* on 11th September. (See page 34.)

FOR THE FALLEN

With proud thanksgiving, a mother for her children,[1]
England mourns for her dead across the sea.
Flesh of her flesh they were, spirit of her spirit,
Fallen[2] in the cause of the free.[3]

Solemn the drums thrill: Death august[4] and royal
Sings sorrow up into immortal spheres.[5]
There is music in the midst of desolation
And a glory that shines upon our tears.

They went with songs to the battle; they were young,
Straight of limb, true of eye, steady and aglow.
They were staunch to the end against odds uncounted:
They fell[6] with their faces to the foe.[7]

They shall grow not old, as we that are left grow old:
Age shall not weary them, nor the years condemn.
At the going down of the sun and in the morning
We will remember them.

They mingle not with their laughing comrades again;
They sit no more at familiar tables of home;
They have no lot[8] in our labour of the day-time;
They sleep beyond England's foam.

But where our desires are and our hopes profound,
Felt as a well-spring that is hidden from sight,
To the innermost heart of their own land they are known
As the stars are known to the Night;

As the stars that shall be bright when we are dust,
Moving in marches upon the heavenly plain;
As the stars that are starry in the time of our darkness,
To the end, to the end they remain.

Lawrence Binyon, published in *The Times*, 21 September, 1914.

1 England's soldiers   2 killed   3 *the free* - the English   4 dignified and impressive   5 *immortal spheres* - Heaven   6 died   7 *faces to the foe* - still fighting, not running away   8 part

FOR ALL WE HAVE AND ARE

For all we have and are,
For all our children's fate,
Stand up and take the war.
The Hun is at the gate![1]
Our world has passed away,
In wantonness o'erthrown,[2]
There is nothing left today
But steel and fire and stone![3]

Though all we knew depart,
The old Commandments stand:−
"In courage keep your heart,
In strength lift up your hand."

Once more we hear the word[4]
That sickened earth of old:−[5]
"No law except the Sword[6]
Unsheathed and uncontrolled."
Once more it knits mankind,[7]
Once more the nations go
To meet and break and bind[8]
A crazed and driven foe.

Comfort, content, delight,
The age's slow-bought gain,
They shrivelled in a night.
Only ourselves remain
To face the naked days[9]
In silent fortitude,
Through perils and dismays[10]
Renewed and re-renewed.

Though all we made depart,
The old Commandments stand:−
"In patience keep your heart,
In strength lift up your hand."

No easy hope or lies
Shall bring us to our goal,
But iron sacrifice[11]
Of body, will, and soul.
There is but one task for all –
One life for each to give.
What stands if Freedom fall?
Who dies if England live?

Rudyard Kipling, 1914

1 *at the gate* - about to attack our homes   2 *wantonness o'erthrown* - lost through foolish living
3 *steel and fire and stone* - fighting, war   4 message, call of duty   5 *That sickened earth of old* -
that in years gone by filled people with doubt and fear   6 *No law except the sword* - force, not
justice, is what counts   7 *knits mankind* - brings people together   8 take captive   9 *naked days* -
comfortless future   10 *perils and dismays* - dangers and disappointments   11 *iron sacrifice* -
sacrifice in war

The stern hand of Fate - the language of a politician

The stern hand of Fate has scourged us to an elevation where we
can see the great everlasting things that matter for a nation – the
great peaks we had forgotten, of Honour, Duty, Patriotism, and,
clad in glittering white, the great pinnacle of Sacrifice pointing
like a great rugged finger to Heaven.

David Lloyd George, Speech at Queen's Hall, reported in *The Times*,
20 September, 1914.

Edward Thomas on war poems

It is the hour of the writer who picks up popular views or phrases,
or coins them, and has the power to turn them into downright
stanzas. Most newspapers have one or more of these gentlemen.
They could take the easy words of a statesman, such as "No price
is too high when honour and freedom are at stake," and dish them
up so that the world next morning, ready to be thrilled by anything
lofty and noble-looking, is thrilled.

Most seem to me bombastic, hypocritical, or senseless; but either
they go straight to the heart of the great public which does not
read poetry, or editors expect them to, and accordingly supply the
articles.

3

THOMAS HARDY 1840 - 1928

EARLY ATTITUDES TO WAR

Before the First World War Hardy seemed to be against war, or at least fully aware of the tragedy and callousness of military conflicts. The outbreak of the Boer War in South Africa (1899-1902) inspired a number of his poems. At the age of fifty-nine he cycled to Southampton to see the troops leave for the war. An added interest for him was the fact that the husband of one of his young lady friends was one of the soldiers leaving.

EMBARCATION

(Southampton Docks: October 1899)

Here, where Vespasian's[1] legions struck the sands,
And Cerdic[2] with his Saxons entered in,
And Henry's[3] army leapt afloat to win
Convincing triumphs over neighbour lands,

Vaster battalions press for further strands,[4]
To argue in the selfsame bloody mode
Which this late age of thought, and pact, and code,[5]
Still fails to mend. – Now deckward tramp the bands,

Yellow as autumn leaves, alive as spring;
And as each host[6] draws out upon the sea
Beyond which lies the tragical To-be,
None dubious of the cause, none murmuring,

Wives, sisters, parents, wave white hands and smile,
As if they knew not that they weep the while.[7]

1 Roman emperor who commanded a legion in Britain   2 Saxon leader who invaded England in 500 A D and founded the Saxon kingdom of Wessex   3 King Henry V beat the French at Agincourt   4 *press for further strands* - hurry to distant shores 5 *pact, and code* - international agreement   6 large numbers of soldiers 7 *they weep the while* - they would soon be weeping

DRUMMER HODGE[1]

They throw in Drummer Hodge, to rest
Uncoffined – just as found:
His landmark is a kopje-crest[2]
That breaks the veldt[3] around;
And foreign constellations west
Each night above his mound.

Young Hodge the drummer never knew –
Fresh from his Wessex home –
The meaning of the broad Karoo,[4]
The Bush, the dusty loam,
And why uprose to nightly view
Strange stars amid the gloam.[5]

Yet portion of that unknown plain
Will Hodge for ever be;
His homely Northern breast and brain
Grow to some Southern tree,
And strange-eyed constellations reign
His stars eternally.

1899

1 Rupert Brooke may have been familiar with this poem. See his sonnet, *The Soldier.*   2 Afrikaans word for a prominent isolated hill in South Africa   3 grasslands   4 high plateaus in South Africa 5 Hardy's version of the word "gloaming" meaning twilight

Between 1904 and 1908 Hardy worked on a massive anti-war poem, *The Dynasts.* In it he wrote: " I have beheld the agonies of war/ Through many a weary season; seen enough/ To make me hold that scarcely any goal/ Is worth the reaching by so red a road."

CHANNEL FIRING

That night your great guns, unawares,
Shook all our coffins as we lay,
And broke the chancel window-squares,
We thought it was the Judgement-day

And sat upright. While drearisome
Arose the howl of wakened hounds:
The mouse let fall the altar-crumb,
The worms drew back into the mounds,

The glebe[1] cow drooled. Till God called, "No;
It's gunnery practice out at sea
Just as before you went below;
The world is as it used to be:

"All nations striving strong to make
Red war yet redder. Mad as hatters
They do no more for Christés sake
Than you who are helpless in such matters.

"That this is not the judgement-hour
For some of them's a blessed thing
For if it were they's have to scour
Hell's floor for so much threatening. . .

"Ha, ha. It will be warmer when
I blow the trumpet (if indeed
I ever do; for you are men,
And rest eternal sorely need)."

So down we lay again. "I wonder,
Will the world ever saner be,"
Said one, "than when He sent us under
In our indifferent century!"[2]

And many a skeleton shook his head.
"Instead of preaching forty year,"
My neighbour Parson Thirdly said,
"I wish I had stuck to pipes and beer."

Again the guns disturbed the hour,
Roaring their readiness to avenge,
As far inland as Stourton[3] Tower,
And Camelot,[4]and starlit Stonehenge.[5]

April, 1914

1 land, especially land adjoining a rectory as part of its property   2 Newspapers often wrote
about the possibility of a war with Germany. This may have added to Hardy's fear of war, and
pessimism about "our indifferent century"   3 possibly the village of Stourton Coundle in
Dorset, England 4 legendary town where the court of King Arthur was situated
5 prehistoric circle of large stone pillars in southern England

WAR PROPAGANDIST

At the age of 74, Thomas Hardy was asked by the British Government
to write in support of the war. He was completely convinced of the jus-
tice of the British cause and of the need to fight. Immediately he set
to work writing patriotic propaganda verse.

MEN WHO MARCH AWAY
(Song of the Soldiers)

What of the faith and fire[1] within us
Men who march away
Ere the barn-cocks say
Night is growing gray,
Leaving all that here can win us;
What of the faith and fire within us
Men who march away?

Is it a purblind prank,[2] O think you,[3]
Friend with the musing eye,[4]
Who watch us stepping by
With doubt and dolorous[5] sigh?
Can much pondering so hoodwink you!
Is it a purblind prank, O think you,
Friend with the musing eye?

Nay. We well see what we are doing,
Though some may not see—
Dalliers[6] as they be—
England's need are we;
Her distress would leave us rueing:
Nay. We well see what we are doing,
Though some may not see!

In our heart of hearts believing
Victory crowns the just,[7]
And that braggarts[8] must
Surely bite the dust,
Press we[9] to the field ungrieving,
In our heart of hearts believing
Victory crowns the just.

Hence the faith and fire within us
Men who march away
Ere the barn-cocks say
Night is growing gray,
Leaving all that here can win us;
Hence the faith and fire within us
Men who march away.

5 September, 1914

---

1 *faith and fire* - trust and absolute determination   2 *purblind prank* - thoughtless silly trick
3 *O think you* - do you think?   4 *with the musing eye* - who looks suspiciously   5 full of pain   6
people who hold back, wait   7 *Victory crowns the just* - people fighting for justice will win   8
bullies   9 *Press we* - we hurry

The children of a "colony" of Belgian refugee workers at their school at Elizabethville.

A response to Belgium's agony

Over a million refugees fled from Belgium in the first two months of the war. A hundred thousand arrived in Britain. Hardy turned his concern for them into poems. The propaganda bureau that Hardy was so keen to support tried especially hard to win over Americans to the British point of view.

ON THE BELGIAN EXPATRIATION

I dreamt that people from the Land of Chimes
Arrived one autumn morning with their bells,
To hoist them on the towers and citadels
Of my own country, that the musical rhymes

Rung by them into space at meted[1] times
Amid the market's daily stir and stress,
And the night's empty star-lit silentness,
Might solace souls of this and kindred climes.

Then I awoke; and lo, before me stood
The visioned ones, but pale and full of fear:
From Bruges they came, and Antwerp, and Ostend.

No carillons in their train. Foes of mad mood
Had shattered these to shards[2] amid the gear
Of ravaged roof, and smouldering gable-end.

18 October, 1914

1 set   2 fragments, pieces

AN APPEAL TO AMERICA ON BEHALF OF THE BELGIAN DESTITUTE

Seven millions stand
Emaciate, in that ancient Delta-land:–
We here, full-charged with our own maimed and dead
And coiled in throbbing conflicts slow and sore,
Can poorly soothe these ails[1] unmerited
Of souls forlorn upon the facing shore!–
Where naked, gaunt, in endless band on band
Seven millions stand.

No man can say
To your great country that, with scant delay,
You must, perforce,[2] ease them in their loud need:
We know that nearer first your duty lies;
But – is it much to ask that you let plead
Your lovingkindness with you – wooing-wise –
Albeit[3] that aught you owe, and must repay,
No man can say?

December, 1914

1 a Thomas Hardy word for ailments   2 necessarily   3 even though

HARDY SUPPORTED THE BRITISH IDEA OF SPORTSMANSHIP IN WAR

To the British press, and the many it influenced, war was a game. It required selfless team work, courage, a willingness to play by the rules. War was an opportunity for heroism, self-sacrifice, patriotism, an opportunity to fight for civilisation, democracy, freedom. It was the greatest game of life that any man could take part in.

Rules could be broken by the British, but when the other side broke a rule then howls of protest were unleashed. It was allowable to take charge of a quarter of the earth's population using guns against spears and bows because that, it was understood, was to bring superior civilisation to the world. It was allowable to blockade German ports to bring starvation to the German people, and continue this action for months after the war was over. It was acceptable for Britain to bomb

Germany but not the other way round. Submarines, used by the Germans to sink ships, were considered an evil. (The Germans sank hundreds of neutral, merchant, and passenger ships.)

The use of poison gas had been outlawed by the First Hague Peace Conference of 1899, so there was a cry of "foul" when the Germans used 168 tonnes of chlorine gas at Langemarck near Ypres, on 22nd April 1915. The next day Kitchener asked the British Cabinet permission for the British army to use poison gas, which it did, for the first time, on 25th September 1915 in the Battle of Loos.

THEN AND NOW

When battles were fought
With a chivalrous sense of Should and Ought,
In spirit men said,
"End we quick or dead,
Honour is some reward!
Let us fight fair — for our own best or worst;
So, Gentlemen of the Guard,
Fire first!"

In the open they stood,
Man to man in his knightlihood:
They would not deign
To profit by a stain
On the honourable rules,
Knowing that practise perfidy no man durst
Who in the heroic schools
Was nurst.

But now, behold, what
Is warfare wherein honour is not!
Rama[1] laments
Its dead innocents:
Herod[2] breathes: "Sly slaughter
Shall rule! Let us, by modes once called accurst,
Overhead, under water,
Stab first."

1915

1 a Hindu god   2 a king in Judea who ordered the slaughter of male babies

HARDY AGAINST CONSCIENTIOUS OBJECTORS

In April 1916 joining the army had become compulsory for all men aged eighteen to forty-one, but many thousands applied for exemption.

A CALL TO NATIONAL SERVICE

Up and be doing, all who have a hand
To lift, a back to bend. It must not be
In times like these that vaguely linger we
To air our vaunts and hopes; and leave our land

Untended as a wild of weeds and sand.
– Say, then, "I come!!" and go, O women and men
Of palace, ploughshare, easel, counter, pen;
That scareless, scathless,[1] England still may stand.

Would years but let me stir as once I stirred
At many a dawn to take the forward track,
And with a stride plunged on to enterprise,

I now would speed like yester wind that whirred
Through yielding pines; and serve with never a slack,
So loud for promptness all around outcries!

March, 1917

1 unharmed, unscathed

REGRETS

WE ARE GETTING TO THE END

We are getting to the end of visioning
The impossible within this universe,
Such as that better whiles may follow worse,
And that our race may mend by reasoning.

We know that even as larks in cages sing
Unthoughtful of deliverance from the curse
That holds them lifelong in a latticed hearse,
We ply spasmodically our pleasuring.

And that when nations set them to lay waste
Their neighbours' heritage by foot and horse,
And hack their pleasant plains in festering seams,[1]
They may again, – not warely,[2] or from taste,
But tickled mad by some demonic force. –
Yes. We are getting to the end of dreams!

Written sometime between 1925 and 1928. One of Hardy's last poems.

1 furrows 2 warily

4

RUPERT BROOKE 1887-1915

BROOKE'S REACTION TO WAR

The group of five sonnets called *1914* that Rupert Brooke wrote in December 1914 and finished in January 1915 became, within a few months, some of the most praised and widely read poems of their day.

They glorified England and the idea of dying for England and one might think that Brooke was very keen to fight and die for his country. In fact, when war broke out in August 1914 Brooke was completely confused. He wrote of his "resentment that he might have to volunteer for military training and service," but he "vaguely imagined a series of heroic feats, vast enterprise, and the applause of crowds."

His feelings reminded him of the time of his mental breakdown which occurred when his girlfriend, Ka (Katherine) Cox, had shown an interest in another young man, the painter, Henry Lamb. After this incident, although he remained on close terms with a number of young women, including the Prime Minister's daughter, Violet Asquith, he never found lasting satisfaction in love. He seemed unable to make a deep personal commitment to anyone. This is reflected in *Peace*, the first of the sonnets. Nor did he seem able to commit himself fully to any ambition or any cause.

Brooke was personally encouraged by Winston Churchill, who was then First Lord of the Admiralty, to join the Royal Naval Division (soldiers under the command of the navy). This he did on 27th September 1914. A week later he went with the navy and gained his only experience of warfare.

For seven days in October Rupert Brooke was in Belgium with his brigade of the Royal Naval Division. He had received almost no training, but was put in charge of a platoon (about 50 men). Their mission was to assist the Belgians in the defence of Antwerp. Massive German guns were pounding the city into ruins and after a few days watching the bombardment Brooke's brigade was ordered to return to England.

He had been, in his own words, "barely under fire," but he had witnessed a city being destroyed, and the people of Antwerp desperately running for their lives as his brigade overtook the refugees to catch trains to Bruges.

He wrote to his friend, the actress, Cathleen Nesbitt:

> We got to a place called Vieux Dieux . . . passing refugees and Belgian soldiers by millions. Every mile the noise got louder, immense explosions and detonations . . . five or six thousand British troops, a lot of Belgians, guns going through, transport wagons, motor cyclists. . . staff officers . . . An extraordinary thrilling confusion.

To another friend, Russell Loines, he wrote, at Christmas, 1914:

> It's all a terrible tragedy. And yet, in it's details, it's great fun. And – apart from the tragedy – I've never felt happier or better in my life than in those days in Belgium.

With his Antwerp experience in mind, unshaken by news of heavy losses on the Western Front in the first months of the war, and with an admiration of military heroism developed at public school, he wrote his series of five sonnets entitled *1914*.

1914

I. PEACE

Now, God be thanked Who has matched us[1] with His hour,
And caught our youth, and wakened us from sleeping,
With hand made sure, clear eye, and sharpened power,
To turn, as swimmers into cleanness leaping,
Glad from a world grown old and cold and weary,
Leave the sick hearts that honour could not move,
And half-men, and their dirty songs and dreary,
And all the little emptiness of love![2]

Oh! we, who have known shame, we have found release[3]
there,
Where there's no ill, no grief, but sleep has mending,
Naught broken save[4] this body, lost but breath;
Nothing to shake the laughing heart's long peace there
But only agony, and that has ending;
And the worst friend and enemy is but Death.

---

1 *matched us* - made us suitable to take part in these thrilling times 2 *emptiness of love* - Brooke was disillusioned with love. He had a stormy relationship with Katherine Cox which led to a nervous breakdown. Other relationships with young women were never lastingly satisfactory.
3 relief, a sense of freedom   4 except

II. SAFETY

Dear! of all happy in the hour, most blest
He who has found our hid security,
Assured in the dark tides of the world at rest,
And heard our word, "Who is so safe as we?"
We[1] have found safety with all things undying,
The winds, and morning, tears of men and mirth,
The deep night, and birds singing, and clouds flying,
And sleep, and freedom, and the autumnal earth.

We have built a house that is not for Time's throwing.[2]
We have gained a peace unshaken by pain for ever.
War knows no power. Safe shall be my going,
Secretly armed against all death's endeavour;
Safe though all safety's lost;[3] safe where men fall;
And if these poor limbs die, safest of all.

1 the soldiers   2 *not for Time's throwing* - not made by Time, or possibly, that Time cannot throw away (suggesting lasting longer than time itself)   3 *Safe though all safety's lost* - nothing can harm them when they are dead.

III. THE RICH DEAD

Blow out, you bugles, over the rich Dead!
There's none of these so lonely and poor of old,[1]
But, dying, has made us rarer gifts than gold.
These laid the world away;[2] poured out the red
Sweet wine of youth; gave up the years to be
Of work and joy, and that unhoped serene,[3]
That men call age; and those who would have been,
Their sons, they gave, their immortality.[4]

Blow, bugles, blow! They brought us, for our dearth,
Holiness, lacked so long, and Love, and Pain.
Honour has come back, as a king, to earth,
And paid his subjects with a royal wage;
And Nobleness walks in our ways again;
And we have come into our heritage.

1 *of old* - from long ago   2 *laid the world away* - perhaps gave up the opportunities life had to offer   3 *unhoped serene* - peaceful old age that some hope not to have to experience   4 quality of living for ever

IV. THE DEAD

These hearts[1] were woven of human joys and cares,
Washed marvellously with sorrow, swift to mirth.
The years had given them kindness. Dawn was theirs,
And sunset, and the colours of the earth.
These had seen movement, and heard music; known
Slumber and waking; loved; gone proudly friended;
Felt the quick stir of wonder; sat alone;
Touched flowers and furs and cheeks. All this is ended.

There are waters blown by changing winds to laughter
And lit by the rich skies, all day. And after,
Frost, with a gesture, stays the waves that dance
And wandering loveliness.[2] He leaves a white
Unbroken glory, a gathered radiance,
A width,[3] a shining peace, under the night.

1 *These hearts* - the opening lines describe the previous emotions and experiences of the now dead
soldiers   2 *wandering loveliness* - Don't look too hard for meaning here   3 *A width* - Brooke may
have lost touch with meaning at this point

V. THE SOLDIER

If I should die, think only this of me:
That there's some corner of a foreign field
That is for ever England. There shall be
In that rich earth a richer dust concealed;[1]
A dust whom England bore, shaped, made aware,
Gave, once, her flowers to love, her ways to roam,
A body of England's, breathing English air,
Washed by the rivers, blest by suns of home.[2]

And think,[3] this[4] heart, all evil shed away,
A pulse in the eternal mind,[5] no less
Gives somewhere back the thoughts by England given;
Her sights and sounds; dreams happy as her day;
And laughter, learnt of friends; and gentleness,
In hearts at peace, under an English heaven.

1 *richer dust concealed* - the buried, dried up remains (dust) of the dead Rupert Brooke   2 *suns
of home* - Brooke is writing as if there were special suns for England, or the sunlight has a
special quality in England   3 just imagine, or think of it this way   4 my   5 *pulse in the eternal
mind* - Brooke's heart, he says, is a pulse beating in God's mind.

BROOKE'S LAST MONTHS

In January 1915, Brooke's *1914* sonnets were published in *New Numbers* (a poetry magazine with a circulation of about 800, run by Brooke and his friends). Events were soon to ensure a greater fame for them.

Brooke's last letters to his friends show him in a range of moods – ecstatically happy, frivolous, resigned, depressed and generally very unsure of the direction of his life.

Whilst working on the *1914* sonnets Brooke had learned that his division was to be sent to fight the Turks in Gallipoli (at the eastern end of the Mediterranean), and that a 75 per cent casualty rate was expected.

On the 10th of January, 1915, he wrote to Dudley Ward,

> We're to be here (in England) till the middle of March, AT LEAST. . . It's too bloody, to have three more months of life, when one hoped for three weeks.

Early in February he wrote to Violet Asquith,

> Oh Violet it's too wonderful for belief. I had not imagined fate could be so benign . . . Do you think perhaps the fort on the Asiatic coast will want quelling . . . and they'll make a sortie and meet us on the plains of Troy? Will Hero's tower crumble under the 15-inch guns? . . . Oh God! I've never been quite so pervasively happy in my life, I think. Never quite so pervasively happy: like a stream flowing entirely to one end. I suddenly realise that the ambition of my life has been - since I was two - to go on a military expedition against Constantinople.

By the 8th of March, a week after sailing for Gallipoli, he seemed not to care about living anymore. He wrote bluntly to Violet Asquith, "Do not care much what happens to me."

The next day he wrote to his old friend and promoter, Winston Churchill's private secretary, Edward Marsh, "I've been such a failure."

And the day after this he wrote to his former girlfriend, Katherine Cox, "It's a good thing I die."

In early April Brooke landed, with his friends, in Egypt where he was slightly unwell. He suffered from sunstroke, and a mosquito bite which was soon to turn septic.

Shortly after this Brooke sailed to the Greek island of Skyros to await final orders for the attack on Gallipoli. As he sailed he wandered up on deck and looked in on his friends with a detached gaze that saw them turning into ghosts before his eyes: and then, at the last moment, he accepted, simply, that he might share their fate. He recorded his experience in his last, barely finished poem, *Soon to Die*. All his fine sounding words have gone and for almost the only time in his life he writes a few lines in blank verse. He coldly faces reality and death.

SOON TO DIE

I strayed about the deck, an hour, to-night
Under a cloudy moonless sky; and peeped
In at the windows, watched my friends at table,
Or playing cards, or standing in the doorway,
Or coming out into the darkness. Still
No one could see me.

        I would have thought of them –
Heedless,[1] within a week of battle – in pity,
Pride in their strength and in the weight and firmness
And link'd beauty of bodies, and pity that
This gay[2] machine of splendour 'ld soon be broken,
Thought little of, pashed, scattered . . .

        Only,[3] always,
I could but see them – against the lamplight – pass
Like coloured shadows, thinner than filmy glass,
Slight bubbles, fainter than the wave's faint light,
That broke to phosphorus[4] out in the night,
Perishing things and strange ghosts – soon to die
To other[5] ghosts – this one, or that, or I.

April, 1915

1 taking no notice   2 wonderful   3 if only   4 catching the light so that the waves appeared to glow or emit light   5 *to other* - to become other

Whilst his ship was anchored off Skyros Brooke became ill with acute blood-poisoning. Within three days he had lost consciousness and died – on 23rd April. His friends, Arthur Asquith, the Prime Minister's son, and Denis Browne, had been by his side in his final hours.

He was buried on Skyros that same evening, by moonlight, in a beautiful olive grove which he had admired only a few days earlier. At six the next morning the friends who had buried him sailed for Gallipoli.

THE SPECIAL PLACE OF BROOKE'S *1914* SONNETS

These five sonnets had an importance in the First World War that went
far beyond poetry. Brooke's clever use of language made dying for Eng-
land sound like a great privilege and the most joyful thing any young
man could do. The sonnets expressed ideas that the nation wanted to be-
lieve. And they were quickly brought to the attention of the entire nation
after Brooke's death by leaders who understood their value as
propaganda.

In his sermon on Easter Sunday, 4th April, in St Paul's Cathedral, Dean
Inge quoted *The Soldier*. This in itself amounted to little, but the ser-
mon was reported in *The Times*. Then, following Brooke's timely death
on 23rd April, glowing obituaries were written, including one, publish-
ed in *The Times,* by the First Lord of the Admiralty himself.

Winston Churchill wrote of Rupert Brooke:

> The thoughts to which he gave expression in the very few
> incomparable war sonnets which he has left behind will be shared
> by the many thousands of young men moving resolutely and
> blithely forward into this, the hardest, the cruellest, and the
> least-rewarding of all wars that men have fought. They are a
> whole history and revelation of Rupert Brooke himself. Joyous,
> fearless, versatile, deeply instructed, with classic symmetry of
> mind and body, ruled by high undoubting purpose, he was all that
> one could wish England's noblest sons to be.

The words, "If I should die" tuned in to thoughts in every soldier's head,
and the reward, patriotic and modest, (decomposing to "a richer dust . . .
which is for ever England") somehow, in the dizzy cold-sweat of the
times, seemed to simple Englishmen, quite adequate.

Patriotism was, once again, seen as a willingness to die for one's coun-
try, not to live for it. Brooke's war sonnets were soon published as *1914
and Other Poems*. The volume was an enormous success, being re-
printed, on average, every eight weeks from May 1915 to October 1918.

COMMENTS ON THE POETRY OF RUPERT BROOKE

Siegfried Sassoon on Brooke

> Rupert Brooke was miraculously right when he said, "Safe shall
> be my going, Secretly armed against all death's endeavour; Safe
> though all safety's lost". He described the true soldier-spirit —
> saint and hero like Norman Donaldson and thousands of others
> who have been killed and died happier than they lived.

Sassoon's diary, 1 April, 1916

Immediately after this entry in his diary Sassoon wrote the poem, *Peace*, which is printed on page 115.

Charles Sorley on Brooke

He is far too obsessed with his own sacrifice, regarding the going to war of himself (and others) as a highly intense, remarkable and sacrificial exploit, whereas it is merely the conduct demanded of him (and others) by the turn of circumstances, where non-compliance with this demand would have made life intolerable. It was not that "they" gave up anything of that list he gives in one sonnet: but that the essence of these things had been endangered by circumstances over which he had no control, and he must fight to recapture them. He has clothed his attitude in fine words: but he has taken the sentimental attitude.

Edward Thomas on Brooke

(Brooke's) sonnets about him enlisting are probably not very personal but a nervous attempt to connect with himself the very widespread idea that self-sacrifice is the highest self-indulgence.

He couldn't mix his thought or the result of it with his feeling. He could only think about his feeling. Radically, I think, he lacked power of expression. He was a rhetorician, dressing things up better than they needed.

Jon Silkin on Brooke

He became increasingly committed, if that is the correct word, to a public and vacant attitude. The two are not necessarily synonymous, but where the poetry is void of personal conviction, it is unlikely to be more than oratory. Brooke's output became poetic oratory. Brooke's sonnets are 'war poems' - *The Soldier*, especially - in the sense that they are vehicles for imperialist attitudes.

Bernard Bergonzi on Brooke

The sonnets themselves are not very amenable to critical discussion. They are works of very great mythic power, since they formed a unique focus for what the English felt, or wanted to feel, in 1914-15: they crystallize the powerful archetype of Brooke, the young Apollo, in his sacrificial role of the hero-as-victim. Considered too, as historical documents, they are an index to the popular state of mind in the early part of the war.

5

CHARLES SORLEY 1895-1915

EDUCATED TO LOVE WAR

Charles Sorley, who was one of the youngest poets to die in the war, was a very unusual young man in August 1914 because he disageed strongly with the idea of fighting Germany. Yet only two years earlier, as a student at Marlborough College, he had accepted completely the public school attitude to war. At that time, as his poetry shows, he believed that to fight and kill for your country was a great and exciting duty.

From A CALL TO ACTION

A thousand years have passed away,
Cast back your glances on the scene,
Compare this England of today
With England as she once has been.

Fast beat the pulse of living then:
The hum of movement, throb of war
The rushing mighty sound of men
Reverberated loud and far.

They girt their loins[1] up and they trod
The path of danger, rough and high;
For Action, Action was their god,
"Be up and doing," was their cry.

***

We, dull and dreamy, stand and blink,
Forgetting glory, strength and pride,
Half-listless watchers on the brink,
Half-ruined victims of the tide.

***

Yes, still we ponder, pry[2], infer,[3]
Decide – and do not DO the same;

Still shrink from action, still prefer
To watch, instead of play, the game.

***

A few have learned the lesson: they
Can never know the good they do;
They help their brethren[4] on their way,
They fight and conquer:– all too few.

Charles Sorley, age 17
Written at Marlborough College, October, 1912.

1 *girt their loins* - literally: wore a cloth round their middle, but suggesting "got themselves ready to fight"   2 look into things, especially where such action is not welcome   3 make judgements
4 brothers

That same month Sorley wrote a bloodthirsty poem, *The Massacre*. In it he recognises that ideas of right and wrong are reversed in war. The fact that the poem was published in the college magazine tells us something about the college's attitude to war and violence. Here are two of the four verses:

From THE MASSACRE

Now Vengeance is greater than Pity,
And Falsehood[1] is mightier than Honour,
And Evil is fairer than Virtue,
And Cursing is sweeter than Prayer:
So plunder, dismantle the city,
And bring desolation[2] upon her,
Nor heed what may harm nor may hurt you,
But leave not a living soul there!

And from every house there was pouring
In torrents a deep crimson flood;
And down every street there was roaring
A wonderful river of blood.
And never a soul felt abhorrence[3]
At this misery, murder and pain;
But the soldiers were drinking the torrents
And quaffing[4] the blood of the slain!

October, 1912

1 lies   2 destruction everywhere   3 shock, repulsion   4 drinking

During the year before the war Charles Sorley was in Germany studying. He had developed a great liking for German people and an admiration for their way of life.

When war was declared Sorley was still in Germany. He was arrested in Trier and put in prison for eight hours. On his release he returned to Cambridge and joined the army at the first opportunity.

SORLEY'S FIRST ATTITUDES TO A REAL WAR

He hated the jingoism which he found everywhere.

> England, I am sick of the sound of the word. In training to fight for England, I am training to fight for that deliberate hypocrisy, that terrible middle-class sloth of outlook and appalling "imaginative indolence" that has marked us out from generation to generation.

He despised himself for submitting to the pressure of public opinion.

> What a worm one is under the cartwheels – big, careless lumbering cartwheels of public opinion. I might have been giving my mind to fight against Sloth and Stupidity: instead, I am giving my body (by a refinement of cowardice) to fight against the most enterprising nation in the world.

He also wrote, a few days after his arrival in Cambridge,

> Isn't all this bloody? I am full of mute and burning rage and annoyance and sulkiness about it. I could wager that out of twelve million eventual combatants there aren't twelve who really want it.

ALL THE HILLS AND VALES

All the hills and vales along
Earth is bursting into song,
And the singers are the chaps
Who are going to die perhaps.
O sing, marching men,
Till the valleys ring again.
Give your gladness to earth's keeping,
So be glad, when you are sleeping.

Cast away regret and rue,
Think what you are marching to.
Little live, great pass.[1]
Jesus Christ and Barabbas
Were found the same day.
This died, that went his way.

    So sing with joyful breath.
    For why, you are going to death.
    Teeming earth will surely store
    All the gladness that you pour.

Earth that never doubts nor fears,
Earth that knows of death not tears,
Earth that bore with joyful ease
Hemlock for Socrates,[2]
Earth that blossomed and was glad
'Neath the cross that Christ had,
Shall rejoice and blossom too
When the bullet reaches you.

    Wherefore,[3] men marching
    On the road to death, sing!
    Pour your gladness on earth's head,
    So be merry, so be dead.

From the hills and valleys earth
Shouts back the sound of mirth,
Tramp of feet and lilt of song
Ringing all the road along.
All the music of their going,
Ringing swinging glad song-throwing,
Earth will echo still, when foot
Lies numb and voice mute.

    On, marching men, on
    To the gates of death with song.
    Sow your gladness for earth's reaping
    So you may be glad, though sleeping.
    Strew your gladness on earth's bed,
    So be merry, so be dead.

August(?), 1914

---

1 passing, death 2 *Hemlock for Socrates* - Socrates was a thinker in Ancient Greece who was
sentenced to death by drinking hemlock which is a poison 3 because of this

At the start of the war many soldiers were filled with a wild happiness at the thought of going to war and beating the Germans. Sorley found their behaviour very difficult to understand and expressed the irony of this in his poem, *All the Hills and Vales*. – Members of D Company, 10th Battalion Royal Fusiliers at Colchester in 1914.

TO GERMANY

You are blind like us. Your hurt no man designed,
And no man claimed the conquest of your land.
But gropers both[1] through fields of thought confined
We stumble and we do not understand.
You only saw your future bigly planned,
And we, the tapering paths of our own mind,
And in each other's dearest ways we stand,
And hiss and hate. And the blind fight the blind.

When it is peace, then we may view again
With new-won eyes each other's truer form
And wonder. Grown more loving-kind and warm
We'll grasp firm hands and laugh at the old pain,
When it is peace. But until peace, the storm
The darkness and the thunder and the rain.

August(?), 1914

1 *gropers both* - both nations tried to understand the situation but both had limited vision

At the end of August Sorley joined the Seventh Battalion of the Suffolk Regiment and went into training at Churn in Berkshire. The battalion moved to Shorncliffe near Folkestone to continue training at the end of September.

A HUNDRED THOUSAND MILLION MITES

A hundred thousand million mites[1] we go
Wheeling and tacking[2] o'er the eternal plain,[3]
Some black with death — and some are white with woe.
Who sent us forth? Who takes us home again?

And there is sound of hymns of praise — to whom?
And curses — on whom curses? — snap the air.
And there is hope goes hand in hand with gloom,
And blood and indignation and despair.

And there is murmuring of the multitude
And blindness and great blindness, until some
Step forth and challenge blind Vicissitude[4]
Who tramples on them: so that fewer come.

And nations, ankle-deep in love or hate,
Throw darts or kisses[5] all the unwitting[6] hour
Beside the ominous[7] unseen tide of fate;[8]
And there is emptiness and drink and power.

And some are mounted on swift steeds[9] of thought
And some drag[10] sluggish feet of stable toil.
Yet all, as though they furiously sought,
Twist turn and tussle, close and cling and coil.

A hundred thousand million mites we sway
Writhing and tossing on the eternal plain,
Some black with death — but most are bright with Day!
Who sent us forth? Who brings us home again?

September, 1914

1 very tiny eight-legged creatures smaller than fleas   2 *Wheeling and tacking* - circling or zigzagging like armies or sailing boats 3 *eternal plain* - everlasting battlegrounds 4 changes of luck 5 *darts or kisses* - make threatening moves or show affection   6 not understanding, a time when neither side understands each other 7 worrying, threatening 8 chance, luck 9 literally horses: some move, or think, quickly   10 move or think slowly

SORLEY'S LAST YEAR

Early in 1915 Sorley wrote to his twin brother, Kenneth,

> Somehow one never lives in the future now, only in the past,
> which is apt to be morbid and begins to make one like an old man.
> The war is a chasm in time. I do wish that all journalists etc, who
> say that war is an ennobling purge etc, etc, could be muzzled. It
> simply makes people unhappy and uncomfortable, if that is a good

thing. All illusions about the splendour of war will, I hope, be gone after the war.

In May 1915 Sorley arrived in France.

SUCH IS DEATH

Such, such is Death: no triumph: no defeat:
Only an empty pail, a slate rubbed clean,
A merciful putting away of what has been.

And this we know: Death is not Life effete,[1]
Life crushed, the broken pail. We who have seen
So marvellous things know well the end not yet.

Victor and vanquished are a-one[2] in death:
Coward and brave: friend, and foe. Ghosts do not say
"Come, what was your record when you drew breath?"
But a big blot has hid each yesterday
So poor, so manifestly[3] incomplete.
And your bright Promise,[4] withered long and sped,[5]
Is touched, stirs, rises, opens and grows sweet
And blossoms and is you, when you are dead.

12 June, 1915

1 worn out, used up 2 equal 3 clearly, obviously 4 potential, expectations of what you would have become 5 gone away

At the end of August 1915, Sorley, at the age of only twenty, was promoted to the rank of captain.

On 5th October, eight days before he was killed, he wrote:

> I dread my own censorious self in the coming conflict. – I also have a great physical dread of pain ... Pray that I ride my frisky nerves with a cold and steady hand when the time arrives.

The following poem was found in Sorley's kit following his death in France.

WHEN YOU SEE MILLIONS OF THE MOUTHLESS DEAD

When you see millions of the mouthless[1] dead
Across your dreams in pale battalions go,
Say not soft things[2] as other men have said,
That you'll remember. For you need not so.
Give them not praise. For, deaf, how should they know
It is not curses heaped on each gashed head?
Nor tears. Their blind eyes see not your tears flow.
Nor honour. It is easy to be dead.
Say only this, "They are dead." Then add thereto,
"Yet many a better one has died before."
Then, scanning all the o'ercrowded mass, should you
Perceive one face that you loved heretofore,[3]
It is a spook.[4] None wears the face you knew.
Great death has made all his for evermore.

September/October, 1915

1 silent mouths stopped by death   2 *soft things* - fine sounding words   3 before this time   4 ghost, something you have imagined

Charles Sorley was killed at the age of twenty on 13th October 1915, in the Battle of Loos.

6

HOME FRONT

BRITAIN TRANSFORMED

A whole way of life in Britain was rapidly changed as the country organised itself for all-out war. Life was filled with new excitement and purpose. Women took on many of the tasks traditionally performed by men and thousands of women volunteered as nurses. Tens of thousands of men and women worked in war-production – making weapons, explosives, tents, boots, uniforms, lorries and all the goods that armies need to survive and fight. Certain foods were in short supply and prices rose rapidly. Newspaper sales boomed.

YOUR COUNTRY NEEDS YOU

> Patriots always talk of dying for their country, and never of killing for their country.
>
> Bertrand Russell

There was a great rush of volunteers at the start. Millions of men left work, or unemployment, to join the army. Fifteen per cent of all recruitment in the war took place in the first two months, but the flow of volunteers was never at anything like this level again. Fewer men enlisted in October than in the first four days of September. But for months recruitment remained at a very high level, stimulated by sympathy for the plight of Belgium – with thousands of Belgian refugees in London by October 1914, and the steady stream of small but alarming attacks the Germans made directly against the citizens of Britain.

In December 1914 German battleships fired on the east coast towns of Scarborough, Whitby, and Hartlepool killing forty civilians and wounding several hundred. In January Zeppelins went into action bombing Yarmouth and Kings Lynn in Norfolk. Zeppelins and aeroplanes continued to drop bombs on England, killing 300 people a year. Ships carrying raw materials and food supplies to Britain were sunk by German submarines.

Over four years, the Germans sent thousands of British ships and millions of tons of foodstuff and supplies to the bottom of the sea.

The poets and verse writers who were popular with newspaper editors were the ones who encouraged men to fight.

FALL IN

What will you lack, sonny, what will you lack
When the girls line up the street,
Shouting their love to the lads come back
From the foe they rushed to beat?
Will you send a strangled cheer to the sky
And grin till your cheeks are red?
But what will you lack when your mate goes by
With a girl who cuts you dead?[1]

Where will you look, sonny, where will you look
When your children yet to be
Clamour to learn of the part you took
In the war that kept men free?
Will you say it was naught to you if France
Stood up for her foe or bunked?[2]
But where will you look when they give the glance
That tells you they know you funked?[3]

How will you fare, sonny, how will you fare
In the far-off winter night,
When you sit by the fire in an old man's chair
And your neighbours talk of the fight?
Will you slink away,[4] as it were from a blow,
Your old head shamed and bent?
Or – say I was not with the first to go,
But I went, thank God, I went?

Why do they call, sonny, why do they call?
For men who are brave and strong?
Is it naught to you if your country fall?
And Right is smashed by Wrong?
Is it football still and the picture show,
The pub and betting odds,
When your brothers stand to the tyrant's blow[5]
And England's call is God's?

Harold Begbie

1 *cuts you dead* - makes a special point of ignoring you 2 ran away 3 were a coward 4 *slink away* - go away in shame, hoping not to be noticed 5 *tyrant's blow* - an attack by an oppressive (bullying) leader (and his country)

The need for more soldiers

It was easy for continental countries to find men for their armies. The soldiers were all there on the orders of their governments. The British army consisted *entirely* of volunteers. As hundreds of thousands of men were killed and wounded more and more volunteers were needed. The height limit was reduced and the upper age limit increased. The flow of recruits continued but it was not sufficient.

Conscription

If the war was to be continued the Government had only one choice: to introduce conscription, which it did in January 1916 with the Military Service Act – calling up all unmarried men aged 18-41 (except those in exempted occupations). On 26th April the Act was extended to include married men.

Pacifists campaigned to persuade men not to fight. This is a piece of propaganda from the pacifist organisation, The Peace Pledge Union.

CONSCIENTIOUS OBJECTION

The Military Service Act put many who opposed the war into a position of direct personal conflict with the Government. Exemption was allowed on grounds of conscience and unsympathetic tribunals were set up to assess those who claimed conscience as a reason for not fighting. Lloyd George promised the conscientious objectors, "a rough time." However, by 1916 many people disagreed with the war and three quarters of a million men gave reasons why they should not fight. The tribunals accepted 16,500 of them as conscientious objectors. The great majority of these agreed to some form of alternative service, but over one thousand refused all forms of service. These were imprisoned and most were brutally treated, resulting in physical and mental abuse and the deaths of some seventy men in prison.

Newspapers campaigned against conscientious objectors. Quakers were well known for their conscientious objection, and were a natural target for Harold Begbie's verse.

A CHRISTIAN TO A QUAKER[1]

I much regret that I must frown
Upon your cocoa nibs;[2]
I simply hate to smite you down
And kick you in the ribs;

But since you will not think as I,
It's clear you must be barred,[3]
So in you go (and may you die)
To two years hard.[4]

We are marching to freedom and to love;
We're fighting every shape of tyrant sin;[5]
We are out to make it worth
God's while to love the earth,
And damn it, you won't join in!

To drive you mad, as I have done,
Has almost made me sick.
To torture Quakers like a Hun
Has hurt me to the quick.
But since your logic wars with mine
You're something I must guard,
So in you go, you dirty swine,
To two years hard.

We are marching to destroy the hosts of hate:
We've taken, every man, a Christian vow;
We are out to make war cease,
That men may live at peace,
And, damme, you're at it now!

Harold Begbie

1 member of the Religious Society of Friends, a society based on the teachings of Christ   2 *cocoa nibs* - a reference to Cadbury, a prominent Quaker family   3 stopped or imprisoned   4 hard labour 5 *tyrant sin* - aggression, atrocity, evil

HOW NEWSPAPERS SUPPORTED THE WAR

British newspapers played an important part in influencing poetry in the First World War. The stories they told about what was happening in the conflict misled ordinary people in Britain and deeply angered soldiers and soldier poets like Sassoon, Owen, and West, fighting in France.

People are not usually keen to risk their lives fighting foreigners. If any government wants its country to fight a war it has to persuade most of its people to fight and to suffer, for months or even years, and millions must be persuaded to risk their lives. To do this it must make people believe that they and their children are threatened, that the enemy is evil, and that their own country is good and fighting in a good cause.

To convince people a government at war does everything it can to spread frightening stories about the enemy and stories which show the enemy is to blame for the war.

From the beginning of the war to the end, every national daily newspaper in Britain co-operated with the Government by telling the news the way the Government wanted it to be told. Their message was that the Germans were evil and must be stopped whatever the cost. They wrote everything they could to convince people to work, fight, sacrifice their sons and husbands and to die in the struggle against Germany.

Some newspaper owners were good friends of leading politicians. The richest and most powerful newspaper owners were the Harmsworth brothers: Lord Northcliffe and Lord Rothermere. Northcliffe owned *The Times* (circulation in 1914, 183,000) and the *Daily Mail* (circulation in 1914, just under a million). Rothermere owned the *Daily Mirror*, the *Sunday Pictorial*, and the *Glasgow Daily Record*. Both owned many local newspapers.

Although politicians knew that newspaper owners supported the war they wanted a direct way to control the news, ideas and opinions presented to the British people. They did this in two ways.

Censorship and control

First, they made sure the army gave very little information about the fighting to the newspapers and no reporters were allowed into France in the first months of the war.

Second, they passed a law — the Defence of the Realm Act — which layed down rules about the kinds of facts and stories they would allow to be printed. No news could be printed which might encourage people to give up the struggle, nor any which made them think that little further effort was needed. Nothing could be printed which might put men off volunteering to fight. If a newspaper had a story it was not sure would meet the guidelines it had to pass it to a new government censorship office, the Press Bureau, for approval.

With such restrictions the newspapers were desperately short of good stories. It is not surprising that they were tempted to invent and exaggerate what they reported. So long as they showed the enemy as a barbarian and the British soldiers as gentlemanly, fair, moderate and always suffering nothing worse than minor setbacks then the Government and its censors at the Press Bureau were content. Newspapers went to extremes of racial hatred.

RACISM

Throughout the country demonstrations and riots erupted; German-owned shops were smashed up.

Only two kinds of people

However the world pretends to divide itself, there are only two divisions in the world today – human beings and Germans.

Rudyard Kipling in the *Morning Post*, 22 June, 1915.

In praise of hatred

> Hatred, or, if my critics prefer it, righteous wrath, is the means to attain invincible resolve and it is as such that I recommend it. Lukewarm feelings can give only half-hearted results.

> Arthur Conan Doyle in *The Times*, 16 January, 1918.

Throughout the war newspapers published stories and opinions which were wildly racist. The politicians did nothing to discourage such racism because they believed it encouraged the war effort. It also encouraged lawless behaviour in Britain. The most prominent of the racist papers was *John Bull*, owned and edited by Horatio Bottomley.

On 7th May 1915 a German submarine sank an "innocent" British passenger liner, *The Lusitania*, in the war zone which it had declared round the British Isles, which then included the whole of Ireland. (There was, in fact, ammunition in the *Lusitania's* cargo.) The Germans had warned of the risks of sailing in the war zone.

From the firing of the first of two torpedoes it took the *Lusitania* just twenty minutes to sink. One thousand one hundred and ninety eight passengers perished including 291 women, and 94 children. The dead included 128 Americans. Many of the bodies washed up on the south coast of Ireland.

What struck the public, encouraged, by the newspapers, was the horror of the civilian losses. It presented a wonderful opportunity for propagandists like Horatio Bottomley to lash the evil Germans for their monstrous act. The press campaign incited rioting, and looting of German shops and property.

> I call for a vendetta - a vendetta against every German in Britain – whether "naturalised" or not . . . You cannot naturalise an unnatural abortion, a hellish freak. But you can exterminate him.

> We have been very patient – patient with the Government, patient with the enemy . . . thousands and thousands of German savages are roaming at large in our midst – and all the time our brave honourable soldiers are being asphyxiated in the trenches; our wounded are being tortured; prisoners are being starved and insulted; unfortified towns are being bombarded; peaceful civilians – old men, women and children – are being murdered; trawlers and merchant vessels are being sunk; and now comes the crowning infamy of the *Lusitania* . . .

> I should welcome the formation of a National Council of Righteous Retribution – a National Vendetta, pledged to

exterminate every German-born man (God forgive the term!) in Britain – and to deport every German-born woman and child . . .

As regards naturalised Germans they should be registered, made to report themselves every day, and compelled to wear a distinctive badge.

Horatio Bottomley in John Bull, 15 May, 1915.

HOW *THE TIMES* REPORTED THE BATTLE OF THE SOMME

The first day of The Battle of the Somme, 1st July 1916, is famous as the greatest disaster in British military history. Twenty thousand British men were killed on that first day, forty thousand were wounded. On 3rd July *The Times* stated in a preliminary report,

EVERYTHING HAS GONE WELL . . . Our troops have successfully carried out their missions, all counter-attacks have been repulsed and large numbers of prisoners taken.

COMPLETE SUCCESS

A further report in *The Times* of 4th July came from "Our Special Correspondent, Press Camp, July 2." The report included these words,

FIRST DAY'S RESULTS

It is now possible to get something like an accurate picture of the results of the first day's fighting in the battle which is now raging here; and the essential fact that stands out is that on the main part of the offensive both we and the French co-operating on our right won complete success . . .

The success of the advance on this main section of the front is most heartening. The enemy's losses at Fricourt and Montauban are known to have been immense.

OUR CASUALTIES

Today I have seen large numbers of German prisoners, including one batch of 470 at a single place. In all it is believed that to date we have taken about 3,000. I have also visited some of our wounded in the collecting stations. They are extraordinarily cheery and brave. It is gratifying to know (and I have gathered the same information at too many points to have any doubt of its accuracy) that an exceptionally large proportion of our casualties are very slight wounds, being injuries from shrapnel and machine-gun fire. Whatever our total casualties may be, the proportion of permanent disablements will be very small. . .

THE EFFECT OF NEWSPAPERS ON THE PUBLIC

In mid 1916 the general public had no way of knowing the facts, and armchair poets could go on imagining our gallant soldiers gloriously fighting for Justice, Right and Freedom. In this way the newspapers, censors and propagandists sent thousands of men to their deaths; or as they might say, in this way they won the war.

THE VISION SPLENDID

Here − or hereafter − you shall see it ended,
This mighty work[1] to which your souls are set;[2]
If from beyond[3] − then, with the vision splendid,
You smile back and never know regret.

Be this your vision! − through you, Life transfigured,
Uplift, redeemed from its forlorn estate,[4]
Purged of the stains[5] which once its soul disfigured,
Healed and restored, and wholly consecrate.

Christ's own rich blood, for healing of the nations,
Poured through his heart the message of reprieve;
God's holy martyrs built on His foundations,
Built with their lives and died that Life might live.

Now, in their train,[6] your blood shall bring like healing;[7]
You, like the Saints, have freely given your all,
And your high deaths, God's purposes revealing,
Sound through the earth His mighty Clarion[8] Call.

O, not in vain has been your great endeavour;
For, by your dyings, Life is born again,
And greater love hath no man tokened[9] ever,
Than with his life to purchase Life's high gain.[10]

John Oxenham, published March, 1917

1 *mighty work* - beating the Germans   2 *souls are set* - minds are made up   3 Heaven
4 condition   5 evils, wrongs   6 *in their train* - following their example   7 *like healing* - similar
healing   8 clear, ringing   9 shown, given   10 *Life's high gain* - Heaven

The following verses, the hymn, *For the Men at the Front*, are reputed to have sold eight million copies during the war.

HYMN: FOR THE MEN AT THE FRONT

Lord God of Hosts, whose mighty hand
Dominion holds on sea and land,
In Peace and War Thy Will we see
Shaping the larger liberty.
    Nations may rise and nations fall,
    Thy Changeless Purpose rules them all.

When Death flies swift on wave or field,
Be Thou a sure defence and shield!
Console and succour those who fall,
And help and hearten each and all!
    O, hear a people's prayers for those
    Who fearless face their country's foes!

For those who weak and broken lie,
In weariness and agony –
Great Healer, to their beds of pain
Come, touch, and make them whole again!
    O, hear a people's prayers, and bless
    Thy servants in their hour of stress!

For those to whom the call shall come
We pray Thy tender welcome home.
The toil, the bitterness, all past,
We trust them to Thy Love at last.
    O, hear a people's prayers for all
    Who, nobly striving, nobly fall!

John Oxenham

PICARDY

When the trees blossom again;
When our spirits lighten –
When in quick sun and rain
Once more the green fields brighten;
Each golden flower those fields among,
The hum of thrifting[1] bee,
Will be the risen flower and song
Of Youth's mortality.[2]

When the birds flutter their wings,
When our scars are healing –
When the furry-footed things
At night again are stealing;
When through the wheat each rippling wave,
The fragrance of flower breath
Will bring a message from the grave,
A whispering from death.

When the sweet waters can flow,
When the world's forgetting –
When once more the cattle low
At golden calm sun-setting;
Each peaceful evening's murmur, then,
And sigh the waters give,
Will tell immortal tale of men
Who died that we might live.

John Galsworthy

1 hard working   2 *risen flower and song of Youth's mortality* - symbols of life renewing and continuing after deaths of young men in the war

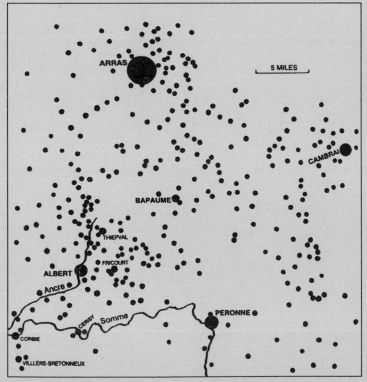

British Commonwealth military cemeteries on the Western Front in an area
approximately thirty miles by thirty five miles.

7

EDWARD THOMAS 1878 - 1917

IN MEMORIAM[1]
(Easter, 1915)

The flowers left thick at nightfall in the wood
This Eastertide call into mind the men,
Now far from home, who, with their sweethearts, should
Have gathered them and will do never again.

6 April, 1915

1 memory

MELANCHOLY

The rain and wind, the rain and wind, raved endlessly.
On me the Summer storm, and fever, and melancholy
Wrought[1] magic, so that if I feared the solitude
Far more I feared all company: too sharp, too rude,
Had been the wisest or the dearest human voice.
What I desired I knew not, but whate'er my choice
Vain it must be, I knew. Yet naught[2] did my despair
But sweeten the strange sweetness, while through the wild air
All day long I heard a distant cuckoo calling
And, soft as dulcimers, sounds of near water falling,
And, softer, and remote as if in history,
Rumours of what had touched my friends, my foes, or me.

25 April, 1915

1 created   2 nothing

ATTRACTED TO SUICIDE

At thirty-seven, Edward Thomas was older than most of the early vol-
unteers, and he was not in the first rush of men to join. For a long time
he could not make up his mind about what action he should take. He

was by nature indecisive, given to moods of great depression and irritability. Death attracted him as a release from his misery. He had once attempted suicide. His enlistment echoed his suicide attempt.

He wrote an account of this event in his short story *The Attempt*. It provides an insight into the workings of his mind. His small daughter had cried when he lost his temper with her.

> Why should he live who had the power to draw such a cry from that sweet mouth? So he used to ask in the luxurious self-contempt which he practised. He would delay no more. He had thought before of cutting himself off from the power to injure his child and the mother of his child. But they would suffer; also, what a rough edge would be left to his life, inevitable in any case, perhaps, but not lightly to be chosen. On the other hand, he could not believe that they would ever be more unhappy than they often were now; at least, the greater poverty which his death would probably cause could not well increase their unhappiness; and settled misery or a lower plane of happiness was surely preferable to a state of faltering hope at the edge of abysses such as he often opened for them. To leave them and not die . . . such a plan had none of the gloss of heroism and the kind of superficial ceremoniousness which was unconsciously much to his taste. But on this day the arguments for and against a fatal act did not weigh with him. He was called to death.
>
> There was also an element of vanity in his project; he was going to punish himself and in a manner so extreme that he was inclined to be exalted by the feeling that he was now about to convince the world he had suffered exceedingly. . . There was little in him left to kill.

Thomas always had financial worries. After the outbreak of the war he was very tempted for a long time to take up the invitation of his friend, the American poet, Robert Frost, to go to America. But after some time he applied for a clerical job at the War Office, and saw his name added to a long list of applicants.

He described his eventual enlistment as, "Not a desperate nor purposed resolution but the natural culmination of a long series of moods and thoughts."

Thomas had a deep love of the English countryside. He walked thousands of miles in it, and had a remarkable knowledge of the natural world. Yet his enlisting was a conscious sacrifice of things he loved, in return for a contentment to be given by Fate. (It was coldly calculated. He was playing Russian roulette.) The following poem he wrote the day of his enlistment.

FOR THESE

An acre of land between the shore and the hills,
Upon a ledge that shows my kingdoms three,
The lovely visible earth and sky and sea
Where what the curlew needs not, the farmer tills:

A house that shall love me as I love it,
Well-hedged, and honoured by a few ash trees
That linnets, greenfinches, and goldfinches
Shall often visit and make love in and flit:[1]

A garden I need never go beyond,
Broken but neat, whose sunflowers every one
Are fit to be the sign of the Rising Sun:
A spring, a brook's bend, or at least a pond:

For these I ask not, but, neither too late
Nor yet too early, for what men call content,
And also that something may be sent
To be contented with, I ask of Fate.

14 July, 1915

1 leave, move house

EDWARD THOMAS AND ELEANOR FARJEON

In the last four years of his life one of Thomas's closest friends was
Eleanor Farjeon. She was a frequent visitor to his family home, and
went on numerous walks with him. He called on her quite often; she
typed all of his poetry for him and sent it off to potential publishers,
who rejected it. Eleanor had fallen in love with Edward Thomas early
in their acquaintance. He, whatever his feelings for Eleanor, was
devoted to his wife, Helen. Eleanor never dared to express her feelings
for Edward because she feared it would instantly bring about the end of
their relationship.

He told her he was enlisting in a letter to her on 15th July 1915. Shortly
after this he called to see Eleanor at her family home. She later wrote
that self torment had gone out of him, and she was glad because of that.

As a tribute to the country he loved, Thomas compiled an anthology of
writing which to him expressed the best qualities of England. In it –
This England, 1915 – he described his reasons for fighting.

It seemed to me that either I had never loved England, or I had
loved it foolishly, aesthetically, like a slave, not having realised

that it was not mine unless I were willing and prepared to die
rather than leave it.

In November 1915 Thomas started his army training at Hare Hall Camp,
Gidea Park, Essex.

THIS IS NO CASE OF PETTY RIGHT OR WRONG

This is no case of petty right or wrong
That politicians or philosophers
Can judge. I hate not Germans, nor grow hot
With love of Englishmen, to please newspapers.
Beside my hate for one fat patriot
My hatred of the Kaiser is love true: –
A kind of god he is, banging a gong.
But I have not to choose between the two,
Or between justice and injustice. Dinned
With war and argument I read no more
Than in the storm smoking along the wind
Athwart[1] the wood. Two witches' cauldrons roar.
From one the weather shall rise clear and gay;
Out of the other an England beautiful
And like her mother that died yesterday.
Little I know or care if, being dull,
I shall miss something that historians
Can rake out of the ashes when perchance[2]
The phoenix[3] broods serene above their ken.
But with the best and meanest Englishmen
I am one in crying, God save England, lest
We lose what never slaves and cattle blessed.
The ages made her that made us from dust:
She is all we know and live by, and we trust
She is good and must endure, loving her so:
And as we love ourselves we hate her foe.

26 December, 1915

1 across   2 perhaps   3 legendary bird that was able to grow again from its own ashes

RAIN

Rain, midnight rain, nothing but the wild rain
On this bleak hut,[1] and solitude, and me
Remembering again that I shall die
And neither hear the rain nor give it thanks
For washing me cleaner than I have been
Since I was born into this solitude.
Blessed are the dead that the rain rains upon:

But here I pray that none whom once I loved
Is dying tonight or lying still awake
Solitary, listening to the rain,
Either in pain or thus in sympathy
Helpless among the living and the dead,
Like a cold water among broken reeds,
Myriads of broken reeds all still and stiff,
Like me who have no love which this wild rain
Has not dissolved except the love of death,
If love it be for what is perfect and
Cannot, the tempest tells me, disappoint.

7 January, 1916

1 probably army hut

NO ONE SO MUCH AS YOU[1]

No one so much as you
Loves this my clay,[2]
Or would lament as you
Its dying day.

You know me through and through
Though I have not told,
And though with what you know
You are not bold.

None ever was so fair
As I thought you:
Not a word can I bear
Spoken against you.

All that I ever did
For you seemed coarse
Compared with what I hid
Nor put in force.

My eyes scarce dare meet you
Lest they should prove
I but respond to you
And do not love.

We look and understand,
We cannot speak
Except in trifles and
Words the most week.

For I at most accept
Your love, regretting
That is all: I have kept
Only a fretting

That could not return
All that you gave
And could not ever burn
With the love you have,

Till sometimes it did seem
Better it were
Never to see you more
Than linger here

With only gratitude
Instead of love –
A pine in solitude
Cradling a dove.

11 January, 1916

1 It has been suggested that this poem may have been addressed to the poet's mother or to his wife (Helen). It seems more likely that it is to his friend, Eleanor Farjeon (who typed all his poems for him) 2 body, flesh

NOW THAT YOU TOO

Now that you too must shortly go the way
Which in these bloodshot years uncounted men
Have gone in vanishing armies day by day,
And in their numbers will not come again:
I must not strain the moments of our meeting
Striving each look, each accent, not to miss,
Or question of our parting and our greeting,
Is this the last of all? Is this? – or this?

Last sight of all it may be with these eyes,
Last touch, last hearing, since eyes, hands, and ears,
Even serving love, are our mortalities,
And cling to what they own in mortal fears: –
But oh, let end what will, I hold you fast
By immortal love, which has no first or last.

Eleanor Farjeon

AND YOU, HELEN

And you, Helen, what should I give you?
So many things I would give you
Had I an infinite great store
Offered me and I stood before
To choose. I would give you youth,
All kinds of loveliness and truth,
A clear eye as good as mine,
Lands, waters, flowers, wine,
As many children as your heart
Might wish for, a far better art
Than mine can be, all you have lost
Upon the travelling waters tossed,
Or given to me. If I could choose
Freely in that great treasure-house
Anything from any shelf,
I would give you back yourself,
And power to discriminate
What you want and want it not too late,
Many fair days free from care
And heart to enjoy both foul and fair,
And myself, too, if I could find
Where it lay hidden and it proved kind.

9 April, 1916

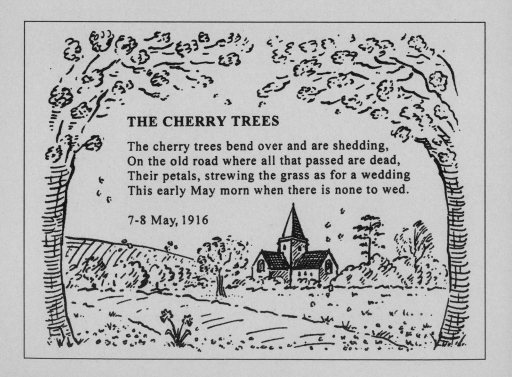

THE CHERRY TREES

The cherry trees bend over and are shedding,
On the old road where all that passed are dead,
Their petals, strewing the grass as for a wedding
This early May morn when there is none to wed.

7-8 May, 1916

NO ONE CARES LESS THAN I

"No one cares less than I,
Nobody knows but God,
Whether I am destined to lie
Under a foreign clod,"
Were the words I made to the bugle call[1] in the morning.

But laughing, storming, scorning,
Only the bugles know
What the bugles say in the morning,
And they do not care, when they blow
The call that I heard and made words to early this morning.

25-26 May, 1916

1 *bugle call* - daily signal to wake up soldiers

AS THE TEAM'S HEAD-BRASS

As the team's[1] head-brass[2] flashed out on the turn
The lovers disappeared into the wood.
I sat among the boughs of the fallen elm
That strewed an angle of the fallow,[3] and
Watched the plough narrowing a yellow square
Of charlock.[4] Every time the horses turned
Instead of treading me down, the ploughman leaned
Upon the handles to say or ask a word,
About the weather, next about the war.
Scraping the share he faced towards the wood,
And screwed along the furrow till the brass flashed
Once more.
            The blizzard felled the elm whose crest
I sat in, by a woodpecker's round hole.
The ploughman said. "When will they take it away?"
"When the war's over." So the talk began –
One minute and an interval of ten,
A minute more and the same interval.
"Have you been out?"   "No."   "And don't want to, perhaps?"
"If I could only come back again, I should.
I could spare an arm. I shouldn't want to lose
A leg. If I should lose my head, why, so,
I should want nothing more . . . Have many gone
From here?"   "Yes."   "Many lost?"   "Yes, a good few.
Only two teams work on the farm this year.
One of my mates is dead. The second day
In France they killed him. It was back in March,
The very night of the blizzard, too. Now if
He had stayed here we should have moved the tree."
"And I should not have sat here. Everything
Would have been different. For it would have been
Another world."   "Ay, and a better, though
If we could see all all might seem good." Then
The lovers came out of the wood again:
The horses started and for the last time
I watched the clods crumble and topple over
After the ploughshare and the stumbling team.

27 May, 1916

1 team of horses   2 *head-brass* - brass decorations traditionally put on the heads of farm horses 3 fallow field (unplanted)   4 a weed also known as wild mustard

THE TRUMPET

Rise up, rise up,
And, as the trumpet blowing
Chases the dreams of men,
As the dawn glowing
The stars that left unlit
The land and water,
Rise up and scatter
The dew that covers
The print of last night's lovers -
Scatter it, scatter it!

While you are listening
To the clear horn,
Forget, men, everything
On this earth new-born,
Except that it is lovelier
Than any mysteries.
Open your eyes to the air
That has washed the eyes of the stars
Through all the dewy night:
Up with the light,
To the old wars;
Arise, arise!

26-28 May, 1916

LIGHTS OUT

I have come to the borders of sleep,
The unfathomable[1] deep
Forest where all must lose
Their way, however straight,
Or winding, soon or late;
They cannot choose.

Many a road and track
That, since the dawn's first crack,
Up to the forest brink,
Deceived the travellers,
Suddenly now blurs,
And in they sink.

Here love ends,
Despair, ambition ends;
All pleasure and all trouble,
Although most sweet or bitter,
Here ends in sleep that is sweeter
Than tasks most noble.

There is not any book
Or face of dearest look
That I would not turn from now
To go into the unknown
I must enter, and leave, alone,
I know not how.

The tall forest towers;
Its cloudy foliage lowers
Ahead, shelf above shelf;
Its silence I hear and obey
That I may lose my way
And myself.

November, 1916

1 not able to be measured, not able to be understood

On the 7th of December Thomas volunteered for France and front line
duties. *Out in the Dark* was his last poem. It was written a month before
embarking for France.

OUT IN THE DARK

Out in the dark over the snow
The fallow fawns invisible go
With the fallow doe;
And the winds blow
Fast as the stars are slow.

Stealthily the dark haunts round
And, when the lamp goes, without sound
At a swifter bound
Than the swiftest hound,
Arrives, and all else is drowned;

And star and I and wind and deer,
Are in the dark together, – near,
Yet far, – and fear
Drums on my ear
In that sage company drear.

How weak and little is the light,
All the universe of sight,
Love and delight,
Before the might,
If you love it not, of night.

24 December, 1916

ELEANOR FARJEON'S FAREWELL TO EDWARD THOMAS

On the 6th of January 1917 Eleanor Farjeon went to the home of Helen and Edward Thomas to see him on his last home leave before going to France. Eleanor knew their parting was "an ending." As he went upstairs to bed she stepped out of her room and said "Good night, Edward," and lifted her face. For the only time in their relationship they kissed. Edward said "Good night" and went to his room.

The next morning, after breakfast, he accompanied Eleanor through Epping Forest part of the way to Loughton Station where they shook hands as usual.

HELEN THOMAS'S FAREWELL

On the 11th of January 1917 Edward Thomas said goodbye to his wife for the last time. Helen said of their parting that she "did not know one could live through such agony."

EDWARD THOMAS'S DEATH

On the 30th of January 1917 Edward Thomas sailed for France. Ten weeks later at the end of the first day of the Battle of Arras on the 9th of April, a German shell narrowly missed him. The shockwave from it stopped his heart and he fell down dead.

8

WOMEN POETS – PART ONE

Many women knew from the start that the war was going to be a great
tragedy. They didn't have to experience it first. Yet other women were
as militaristic and as aggressive as any man.

JOINING THE COLOURS
(West Kents, Dublin, August 1914)

There they go marching all in step so gay!
Smooth-cheeked and golden, food for shells and guns.
Blithely they go as to a wedding day,
The mothers' sons.

The drab street stares to see them row on row
On the high tram-tops, singing like the lark
Too careless-gay for courage, singing they go
Into the dark.

With tin whistles, mouth-organs, any noise,
They pipe the way to glory and the grave;
Foolish and young, the gay and golden boys
Love cannot save.

High heart! High courage! The poor girls they kissed
Run with them: they shall kiss no more, alas!
Out of the mist they stepped – into the mist
Singing they pass.

Katharine Tynan

HE WENT FOR A SOLDIER

He marched away with a blithe young score of him
With the first volunteers,
Clear-eyed and clean and sound to the core of him,
Blushing under the cheers.
They were fine, new flags that swung a-flying there,
Oh, the pretty girls he glimpsed a-crying there,

Pelting him with pinks and with roses –
Billy, the Soldier Boy!

Not very clear in the kind young heart of him
What the fuss was about,
But the flowers and the flags seemed part of him –
The music drowned his doubt.
It's a fine, brave sight they were a-coming there
To the gay, bold tune they kept a-drumming there,
While the boasting fifes shrilled jauntily –
Billy, the Soldier Boy!

Soon he is one with the blinding smoke of it –
Volley and curse and groan:
Then he has done with the knightly joke of it –
It's rending flesh and bone.
There are pain-crazed animals a-shrieking there
And a warm blood stench that is a-reeking there;
He fights like a rat in a corner –
Billy, the Soldier Boy!

There he lies now, like a ghoulish score of him,
Left on the field for dead:
The ground all around is smeared with the gore of him -
Even the leaves are red.
The Thing that was Billy lies a-dying there,
Writhing and a-twisting and a-crying there;
A sickening sun grins down on him –
Billy, the Soldier Boy!

Still not quite clear in the poor, wrung heart of him
What the fuss was about,
See where he lies – or a ghastly part of him –
While life is oozing out:
There are loathsome things he sees a-crawling there;
There are hoarse-voiced crows he hears a-calling there,
Eager for the foul feast spread for them –
Billy, the Soldier Boy!

How much longer, O Lord, shall we bear it all?
How many more red years?
Story it and glory it and share it all,
In seas of blood and tears?
They are braggart[1] attitudes we've worn so long;
They are tinsel platitudes[2] we've sworn so long –
We who have turned the Devil's Grindstone,
Borne with[3] the hell called War!

Ruth Comfort Mitchell

1 boastful   2 *tinsel platitudes* - attractive-sounding, popular, but empty statements   3 *Borne with* -
endured, put up with

WOMEN MAKE BULLETS AND BOMBS

947,000 women were employed in munition work, making bullets and
explosive shells. Three hundred workers lost their lives from T N T poisoning
and from explosions in factories during the war.

A poster designed to entice women to make bombs and bullets. It points to one of the big
questions about war. Is it possible to save life by making the means to destroy life?

WOMEN AT MUNITION[1] MAKING

Their hands should minister unto the flame of life,
Their fingers guide
The rosy teat, swelling with milk,
To the eager mouth of the suckling babe
Or smooth with tenderness,
Softly and soothingly,
The heated brow of the ailing child.
Or stray among the curls
Of the boy or girl, thrilling to mother love.
But now,
Their hands, their fingers
Are coarsened in munition factories.
Their thoughts, which should fly
Like bees among the sweetest mind flowers,
Gaining nourishment for the thoughts to be,
Are bruised against the law,
"Kill, kill."
They must take part in defacing and destroying the natural body
Which, certainly during this dispensation
Is the shrine of the spirit.
O God! – Throughout the ages we have seen,
Again and again
Men by Thee created
Cancelling each other.
And we have marvelled at the seeming annihilation
Of Thy work.
But this goes further,
Taints the fountain head,
Mounts like a poison to the Creator's very heart.
O God! – Must It anew be sacrificed on earth?

Mary Gabrielle Collins

1 manufacture of bombs, bullets and other military equipment

MOTHERS PROUD OF SOLDIER SONS

Those gallant boys of whom we, their mothers, and, I venture to think, the whole British nation are justly proud . . .

If my own son can best serve England at this juncture by giving his life for her, I would not lift one finger to bring him home. If any act or word of mine should interfere with or take from him his grandest privilege, I could never look him in the face again.

Mrs Berridge
in *The Morning Post*, 30 September, 1914.

THE TWO MOTHERS

"Poor woman, weeping as they pass,
Yon brave recruits, the nation's pride,
You mourn some gallant boy, alas!
Like mine who lately fought and died?"

"Kind stranger, not for soldier son,
Of shame, not grief, my heart will break.
Three stalwarts have I, but not one
Doth risk his life for England's sake!"

Matilda Betham-Edwards

THE CALL

Who's for the trench –
Are you, my laddie?
Who'll follow French –[1]
Will you, my laddie?
Who's fretting to begin,
Who's going out to win?
And who wants to save his skin –
Do you, my laddie?

Who's for the khaki suit –
Are you, my laddie?
Who longs to charge and shoot –
Do you my, laddie?
Who's keen on getting fit,
Who means to show his grit,
And who'd rather wait a bit –
Would you, my laddie?

Who'll earn the Empire's thanks –
Will you, my laddie?
Who'll swell the victor's ranks –
Will you, my laddie?
When that procession comes,
Banners and rolling drums –
Who'll stand and bite his thumbs –
Will you, my laddie?

Jessie Pope

1 Sir John French, the first Commander-in-Chief of the British Forces in
France and Belgium in 1914 and 1915

TO THE VANGUARD

Oh, little mighty Force[1] that stood for England!
That, with your bodies for a living shield,
Guarded her slow awaking, that defied
The sudden challenge of tremendous odds
And fought the rushing legions[2] to a stand —
Then stark in grim endurance held the line.
O little Force that in your agony
Stood fast while England girt her armour on,
Held high our honour in your wounded hands,
Carried our honour safe with bleeding feet —
We have no glory great enough for you,
The very soul of Britain keeps your day!
Procession? — Marches forth a Race in Arms;
And, for the thunder of the crowd's applause,
Crash upon crash the voice of monstrous guns,
Fed by the sweat, served by the life of England,
Shouting your battle-cry across the world.

Oh, little mighty Force, your way is ours,
This land inviolate[3] your monument.

Beatrix Brice-Miller

1 *little mighty Force* - the British Expeditionary Force which put up fierce resistance against overwhelming German numbers in August 1914 before being forced to retreat   2 a unit of the Roman army, a term used here poetically to mean the vast German army   3 safe from invaders

TO MY BROTHER
(In memory of July 1st, 1916)

Your battle-wounds are scars upon my heart,
Received when in that grand and tragic "show"[1]
You played your part
Two years ago,

And silver in the summer morning sun
I see the symbol of your courage glow —
That Cross you won
Two years ago.

Though now again you watch the shrapnel fly,
And hear the guns that daily louder grow,
As in July
Two years ago,

May you endure to lead the Last Advance[2]
And with your men pursue the flying foe
As once in France
Two years ago.

Vera Brittain

1 battle 2 *Last Advance* - the final attack of the war

I SHOUTED FOR BLOOD

I shouted for blood as I ran, brother,
Till my bayonet pierced your breast:
I lunged thro' the heart of a man, brother,
That the sons of men might rest.[1]

I swung up my rifle apace,[2] brother.
Gasping with wrath awhile,
And I smote at your writhing face, brother,
That the face of peace might smile.

Your eyes are beginning to glaze,[3] brother,
Your wounds are ceasing to bleed.
God's ways are wonderful ways, brother,
And hard for your wife to read.

Janet Begbie

1 enjoy peace   2 quickly   3 look glassy (dead)

FILMS FOR PROPAGANDA

In December 1915 the Wellington House propagandists launched the
first (silent) propaganda film of the war, *Britain Prepared.* It was
shown in London daily till mid February. In August 1916 the film *The
Battle of the Somme* was showing in thirty London cinemas and had
2000 bookings all over the country by October. The film makers may
have misjudged what people would think when they saw the films.

A WAR FILM

I saw,
With a catch of the breath and the heart's uplifting,
Sorrow and pride, the "week's great draw" –
The Mons Retreat;[1]
The "Old Contemptibles"[2] who fought, and died,
The horror and the anguish and the glory.

As in a dream,
Still hearing machine-guns rattle and shells scream,
I came out into the street.

When the day was done,
My little son
Wondered at bath-time why I kissed him so,
Naked upon my knee.
How could he know
The sudden terror that assaulted me? . .
The body I had borne
Nine moons beneath my heart,
A part of me . . .
If, someday,
It should be taken away
To War. Tortured. Torn.
Slain.
Rotting in No Man's Land, out in the rain –
My little son . . .
Yet all those men had mothers, every one.

How should he know
Why I kissed and kissed and kissed him, crooning his name?
He thought that I was daft.
He thought it was a game,
And laughed, and laughed.

Teresa Hooley

1 *Mons Retreat* - Mons, a town near the western border of Belgium. British forces, heavily
outnumbered by the Germans retreated here in the first month of the war   2 *Old Contemptibles* -
British Army in France in 1914; the Kaiser had described the British Army as a "contemptible little
army"

LOVE AND FAREWELLS

LAST LEAVE (1918)

Let us forget tomorrow! For tonight
At least, with curtains drawn, and driftwood piled
On our own hearthstone, we may rest, and see
The firelight flickering on familiar walls.
(How the blue flames leap when an ember falls!)

Peace, and content, and soul-security –
These are within. Without, the waste is wild
With storm-clouds sweeping by in furious flight,
And ceaseless beating of autumnal rain
Upon our window pane.

The dusk grows deeper now, the flames are low:
We do not heed the shadows, you and I,
Nor fear the grey wings of encroaching gloom,
So softly they enfold us. One last gleam
Flashes and flits, elusive as a dream,
And then dies out upon the darkened room.
So, even so, our earthly fires must die;
Yet, in our hearts, love's flame shall leap and glow
When this dear night, with all it means to me,
Is but a memory!

Eileen Newton

UNDER THE SHADOW

Under the shadow of a hawthorn brake,[1]
Where bluebells draw the sky down to the wood,
Where 'mid brown leaves, the primroses awake
And hidden violets smell of solitude;
Beneath green leaves bright-fluttered by the wing
Of fleeting, beautiful, immortal Spring,
I should have said, " I love you," and your eyes
Have said, "I too. . ." The gods saw otherwise.

For this is winter, and the London streets
Are full of soldiers from that far, fierce fray
Where life knows death, and where poor glory meets
Full-face with shame, and weeps and turns away.
And in the broken, trampled foreign wood
Is horror, and the terrible scent of blood,
And love shines tremulous, like a drowning star,
Under the shadow of the wings of war.

Edith Nesbit, first published December, 1915

1 dense growth of the hawthorn hedge which gives some protection from the wind

IN TIME OF WAR

I dreamed (God pity babes at play)
How I should love past all romance,
And how to him beloved should say,
As heroes' women say, perchance,[1]
When the deep drums awake —
"Go forth: do gloriously for my dear sake."

But now I render, blind with fear,
No lover made of dreams, but You,
O You — so commonplace, so dear,
So knit with all I am or do!
Now, braver thought I lack:
Only God bring you back — God bring you back!

Lesbia Thanet

1 perhaps

9

TRENCH WARFARE

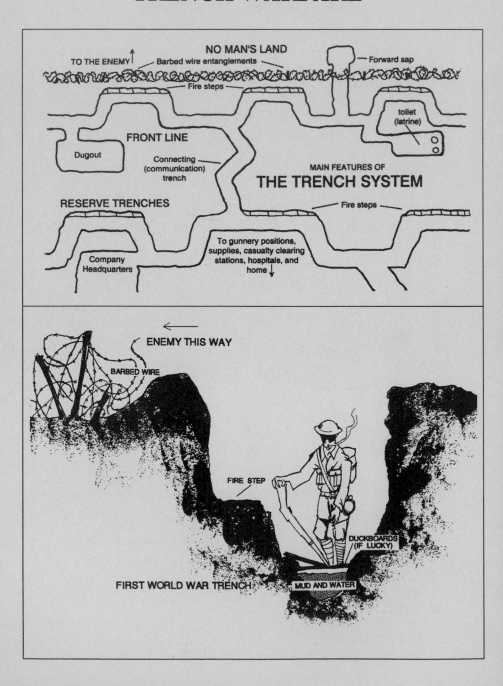

NO MAN'S LAND

TO THE ENEMY Barbed wire entanglements Forward sap

Fire steps

FRONT LINE

Dugout

toilet
(latrine)

Connecting
(communication)
trench

MAIN FEATURES OF
THE TRENCH SYSTEM

RESERVE TRENCHES

Fire steps

Company
Headquarters

To gunnery positions,
supplies, casualty clearing
stations, hospitals, and
home

ENEMY THIS WAY

BARBED WIRE

FIRE STEP

DUCKBOARDS
(IF LUCKY)

FIRST WORLD WAR TRENCH MUD AND WATER

BRITISH MILITARY INTELLIGENCE

Although British schoolboys at the start of the twentieth century had been brought up to think of war and soldiers as great and glorious their thinking was quite unrealistic. They thought of themselves as heroes in Greek myths; and the British army was almost as out-of-date and out of touch with reality.

It had not adjusted to the possibility of an enemy possessing weapons equal to or better than its own. It believed that character was more important than weapons.

Launcelot Kiggell, Chief of Staff of the British Expeditionary Force - the first British army to arrive in France to oppose the Germans, wrote, "The moral has been to the physical as three is to one. Courage, energy, determination, perseverance, endurance, the unselfishness and discipline that make combination possible - these are the primary causes of all great successes, and in turning our thoughts to new guns or rifles or bayonets, we too often forget the fact."

British military leaders should have learned from their experience in the Boer War, 1899-1902, when their army of 450,000 trained soldiers faced 50,000 Boer farmers in South Africa. The British army won, but its performance was abysmal. It cost them 22,000 lives , £200 million and took them three years. They learned nothing from the Boer's effective use of the machine gun and said that the use of trenches by the Boers showed a lack of character: the Boers were not man enough to stand up and fight.

The first British army in France, the British Expeditionary Force soon found itself facing the might of the German army. Simply to survive it started digging trenches in which men could hide from the enemy guns, fire on enemy soldiers and live, waiting for orders either to carry out raids on enemy positions or to take part in an occasional massive attack.

In a matter of months, as many thousands more soldiers arrived, and with the French armies covering the southern sector, over 400 miles of trenches were dug from Belgium, through France almost to the Swiss border.

The Germans took a similar approach, though applied slightly more intelligence, retiring to the highest ground around, and leaving the swamps to the English. In such places the Germans often turned their trenches into bunkers up to 10 metres (about 30 feet) deep, securely built of concrete, and comfortably furnished.

Behind the trenches were the reserves, the supplies, casualty clearing stations and field hospitals, and the commanders. The headquarters were at a safe distance from the war zone. For the Battle of the Somme, Field Marshal Haig conducted the action from Montreuil, fifty miles from the front line.

A 9.2 inch field gun in action. One man attempts to protect his hearing, but thousands were made deaf by such experiences.

MAKING AN ATTACK

Usually, before a major attack, the massive long range guns fired onto the enemy lines for many hours or even day and night for a week or more. This gave the enemy the warning he needed to bring up his reserves and prepare to fight, but the intention was to demolish the enemy front lines, their inhabitants, and the barbed wire entanglements which protected them from foot soldiers.

In the Battle of Passchendaele three thousand heavy guns fired for ten days delivering four and three quarter tons of explosive for every yard of the German front line. The cost of the shells used was twenty-two million pounds.

After the bombardment, in an attempt to overwhelm the enemy, hundreds, and sometimes thousands of men would be ordered out of the trenches ("going over the top") to advance across the open ground of no-man's land. They walked in a line, shoulder to shoulder, carrying their rifles with bayonets fixed, into a blaze of fire from the rifles and machine guns of the enemy. – After many months of unhappy experience with this approach looser formations were used.

A further improvement came when Field Marshal Haig, who considered the machine gun a "much over-rated weapon" and allowed only two per battalion, was overruled by Lloyd George who increased the supply of these weapons.

THIEPVAL WOOD

The tired air groans as the heavies swing over, the river-hollows boom;
The shell-fountains leap from the swamps, and with wild-fire and fume
The shoulder of the chalk down[1] convulses.
Then jabbering echoes stampede in the slatting wood,
Ember-black the gibbet trees like bones or thorns protrude
From the poisonous smoke –   past all impulses.
To them these silvery dews can never again be dear,
Nor the blue javelin-flame of thunderous noons strike fear.

Edmund Blunden, September, 1916

1 hill

Julian Grenfell – A soldier in love with war

Grenfell, who was educated at Eton, loved the barbaric life of a soldier at war. From his comments he would appear to have been a man without conscience or compassion. Perhaps we should consider carefully the moral values expressed in his famous and very popular poem, *Into Battle*.

He wrote,

> I adore war. It's like a big picnic without the objectlessness of a
> picnic. I've never been so well or happy. No one grumbles at one
> for being dirty.
>
> The war just suits my stolid health, and stolid nerves, and barbaric
> disposition. The fighting excitement vitalises everything, every
> sight and word and action. . .
>
> One loves one's fellow-man so much more when one is bent on
> killing him.

His speciality, he revealed in a letter to his parents, was stalking Ger-
man snipers and shooting them from very close range. War gave him
permission and encouragement to do what he loved best.

INTO BATTLE

The naked earth is warm with spring,
And with green grass and bursting trees
Leans to the sun's gaze glorying,
And quivers in the sunny breeze;

And life is colour and warmth and light,
And a striving evermore for these;
And he is dead who will not fight;
And who[1] dies fighting has increase.[2]

The fighting man shall from the sun
Take warmth, and life from the glowing earth;
Speed with the light-foot winds to run,
And with the trees to newer birth;
And find, when fighting shall be done,
Great rest, and fullness after dearth.[3]

All the bright company of Heaven
Hold him in their high comradeship,
The Dog-Star, and the Sisters Seven,
Orion's Belt[4] and sworded hip.

The woodland trees that stand together,
They stand to him each one a friend;
They gently speak in the windy weather;
They guide to valley and ridge's end.

The kestrel hovering by day,
And the little owls that call by night,
Bid him be swift and keen as they,
As keen of ear, as swift of sight.

The blackbird sings to him, "Brother, brother,
If this be the last song you shall sing,
Sing well, for you may not sing another;
Brother, sing."

In dreary, doubtful waiting hours,
Before the brazen frenzy starts,
The horses show him nobler powers;
O patient eyes, courageous hearts!

And when the burning moment breaks,
And all things else are out of mind,
And only joy of battle takes
Him by the throat, and makes him blind,

Through joy and blindness he shall know,
Not caring much to know, that still
Nor lead nor steel[5] shall reach him, so
That it be not the Destined Will.[6]

The thundering line of battle stands,
And in the air Death moans and sings;
But Day shall clasp him with strong hands,
And Night shall fold him in soft wings.

Julian Grenfell

---

1 he who   2 benefit   3 emptiness   4 *Dog -Star, sisters Seven, Orion's Belt* - stars and
constellations   5 *Nor lead, nor steel* - neither bullets nor bayonets   6 *Destined Will* - what fate
(or possibly God) has planned

THE TARGET

I shot him, and it had to be
One of us! 'Twas him or me.
"Couldn't be helped," and none can blame
Me, for you would do the same.

My mother, she can't sleep for fear
Of what might be a-happening here
To me. Perhaps it might be best
To die, and set her fears at rest.

For worst is worst, and worry's done.
Perhaps he was the only son . . .
Yet God keeps still, and does not say
A word of guidance any way.

Well, if they get me, first I'll find
That boy, and tell him all my mind,
And see who felt the bullet worst,
And ask his pardon, if I durst.

All's tangle. Here's my job.
A man might rave, or shout, or sob;
And God He takes no sort of heed.
This is a bloody mess indeed.

Ivor Gurney

PAIN

Pain, pain continual; pain unending;
Hard even to the roughest, but to those
Hungry for beauty[1] . . . Not the wisest knows,
Nor most pitiful-hearted, what the wending
Of one hour's way meant.[2] Grey monotony lending
Weight to the grey skies, grey mud where goes
An army of grey bedrenched scarecrows in rows
Careless at last[3] of cruellest Fate-sending.
Seeing the pitiful eyes of men foredone.[4]
Or horses shot, too tired merely to stir,
Dying in shell-holes both, slain by the mud.
Men broken,[5] shrieking even to hear a gun.
Till pain grinds down, or lethargy[6] numbs her,
The amazed heart cries angrily out on God.

Ivor Gurney

1 *Hungry for beauty* - sensitive men who appreciate the beautiful things in life (Ivor Gurney would have counted himself amongst these men. He was an accomplished musician, and composer as well as poet)   2 *the wending of one hour's way meant* - no-one understands what even one hour of suffering means   3 *Careless at last* - past caring what cruel fate might send   4 doomed to die
5 mentally broken   6 great weariness

NIGHT PATROL

"Over the top![1] The wire's thin here, unbarbed
Plain rusty coils, not staked, and low enough:
Full of old tins, though. — When you're through, all three,
Aim quarter left for fifty yards or so,

Then straight for that new piece of German wire;
See if it's thick, and listen for a while
For sounds of working; don't run any risks;
About an hour; now, over!"
                              And we placed
Our hands on the topmost sand-bags, leapt, and stood
A second with curved backs, then crept to the wire,
Wormed ourselves tinkling through, glanced back, and dropped.
The sodden ground was splashed with shallow pools,
And tufts of crackling cornstalks, two years old,
No man had reaped,[2] and patches of spring grass,
Half-seen, as rose and sank the flares,[3] were strewn
With the wreck of our attack: the bandoliers,[4]
Packs, rifles, bayonets, belts, and haversacks,
Shell fragments, and the huge whole forms of shells
Shot fruitlessly – and everywhere the dead.
Only the dead were always present – present
As a vile sickly smell of rottenness;
The rustling stubble and the early grass,
The slimy pools – the dead men stank through all,
Pungent and sharp; as bodies loomed before,
And as we passed, they stank; then dulled away
To that vague foetor,[5] all encompassing,
Infecting earth and air. They lay, all clothed,
Each in some new and piteous attitude
That we well marked to guide us back; as he,
Outside our wire, that lay on his back and crossed
His legs Crusader-wise; I smiled at that,
And thought of Elia[6] and his Temple Church.
From him, a quarter left, lay a small corpse,
Down in a hollow, huddled as in bed,
That one of us put his hand on unawares.
Next was a bunch of half a dozen men
All blown to bits, an archipelago
Of corrupt[7] fragments, vexing to us three,
Who had no light to see by, save the flares.
On such a trail, so lit, for ninety yards
We crawled on belly and elbows, till we saw,
Instead of lumpish dead before our eyes,
The stakes and crosslines of the German wire.
We lay in shelter of the last dead man,
Ourselves as dead, and heard their shovels ring
Turning the earth, their talk and cough at times.
A sentry fired and a machine-gun spat;
They shot a flare above us, when it fell
And spluttered out in the pools of No Man's Land,
We turned and crawled past the remembered dead;
Past him and him, and them and him, until,
For he lay some way apart, we caught the scent

Of the Crusader and slid past his legs,
And through the wire and home, and got our rum.

Arthur Graeme West

1 *Over the top* - the command to climb out of the trench over the top of the sandbags and take part
in a raid (as here) or an attack   2 harvested   3 military fireworks giving off a bright light, sent up
to show up enemy troop movements   4 soldier's shoulder belt with pockets for ammunition etc
5 foetor, stench, awful smell   6 Charles Lamb   7 rotten

GOD, HOW I HATE YOU

God! how I hate you, you young cheerful men,
Whose pious poetry blossoms on your graves
As soon as you are in them . . .
                          Hark how one chants –
"O happy to have lived these epic days" --
"These epic days!" And *he'd* been to France,
And seen the trenches, glimpsed the huddled dead
In the periscope, hung on the rusty wire:
Choked by their sickly foetor, day and night
Blown down his throat: stumbled through ruined hearths,
Proved all that muddy brown monotony
Where blood's the only coloured thing. Perhaps
Had seen a man killed, a sentry shot at night,
Hunched as he fell, his feet on the firing-step,
His neck against the back slope of the trench,
And the rest doubled between, his head
Smashed like an eggshell and the warm grey brain
Spattered all bloody on the parados[1]. . .
Yet still God's in His Heaven, all is right
In this best possible of worlds . . . God loves us,
God looks down on this our strife
And smiles in pity, blows a pipe at times
And calls some warriors home . . .
                          How rare life is!
On earth, the love and fellowship of men,
Men sternly banded: banded for what end?
Banded to maim and kill their fellow men –
For even Huns are men. In Heaven above
A genial umpire, a good judge of sport
Won't let us hurt each other! Let's rejoice
God keeps us faithful, pens us still in fold.
Ah, what a faith is ours (almost, it seems,
Large as a mustard seed) – we trust and trust,
Nothing can shake us! Ah how good God is
To suffer us to be born just now, when youth

That else would rust, can slake his blade in gore
Where very God Himself does seem to walk
The bloody fields of Flanders[2] He so loves.

Arthur Graeme West

1 the back rim of the trench   2 an area of land partly in France, partly in Belgium where much of
the fighting of the First World War took place

West's doubts

West was an atheist who simply could not understand the Christian
God that his fellow soldiers believed in. He was a man full of doubts.
He volunteered to fight, and later trained as an officer. He was puzzled
by fellow officers whom he described as "worthy and unselfish . . . not
aggressive or offensively military . . . almost the best value in the
upper class that we have . . . " He couldn't understand how they
could, "give so much labour and time to the killing of others, though
to the plain appeals of poverty and inefficiency in government, as
well national as international, they are so absolutely heedless. How is
it that as much blood and money cannot be poured out when it is
a question of saving and helping mankind rather than of slaying
them?"

He toyed with the idea of refusing to fight but lacked the courage to do
so. "No one is willing to revise his ideas or make clear to himself his
motives for joining the war; even if anybody feels regret for having
enlisted, he does not like to admit it to himself. Why should he? Every
man, woman and child is taught to regard him as a hero."

TRAINING FOR BRAVERY

After a dinner party at St Omer in northern France on 4th December
1914, at which King George V was one of the guests, Field Marshal
Haig wrote in his diary,

> The King seemed very cheery but inclined to think that all our
> troops are by nature brave and is ignorant of all the efforts which
> commanders must make to keep up the 'morale' of their men in
> war, and of all the training which is necessary in peace in order
> to enable a company for instance to go forward as an organised
> unit in the face of almost certain death.

DEATH'S MEN

Under a grey October sky
The little squads that drill
Click arms and legs mechanically,
Emptied of ragged will!

Of ragged will that frets[1] the sky
From crags jut ragged pines,
A wayward immortality,
That flies from Death's trim lines.

The men of death stand trim and neat,
Their faces stiff as stone,
Click, clack, go four and twenty feet
From twelve machines of bone.

"Click, clack, left, right, form fours, incline,"
The jack-box[2] sergeant cries;
For twelve erect and wooden dolls
One clockwork doll replies.

And twelve souls wander 'mid still clouds
In a land of snow-drooped trees,
Faint, foaming streams fall in grey hills
Like beards on old men's knees.

Old men, old hills, old kings their beards
Cold stone-grey still cascades
Hung high above this shuddering earth
Where the red blood sinks and fades.

Then the quietness of all ancient things,
Their round and full repose
As balm upon twelve wandering souls
Down from the grey sky flows.

The rooks from out the tall gaunt trees
In shrieking circles pass;
Click, clack, click, clack, go Death's trim men
Across the Autumn grass.

W. J. Turner

1 patterns   2 jack-in-the-box, mechanical

PREPARING TO DIE

I am now dead . . . The last letter of Glyn Rhys Morgan

Whilst waiting for an attack to begin soldiers were often asked to write letters to be sent home in the event of their deaths.

My Dear Dad

This letter is being written on the eve of going "over the top." It is only because I know by this time what are the odds against returning unhurt that I write it. It will only be sent in the event of my being killed in action.

You, I know, my dear Dad, will bear the shock as bravely as you have always borne the strain of my being out here; yet I should like if possible, to help you to carry on with as stout a heart as I hope to "jump the bags."

I believe I have told you before that I do not fear Death itself; the Beyond has no terror for me. I am quite content to die for the cause for which I have given up nearly three years of my life and I only hope that I may meet Death with as brave a front as I have seen other men do before.

My one regret is that the opportunity has been denied me to repay you to the best of my ability for the lavish kindness and devotedness which you have shown me. I had hoped to do so in the struggle of Life. Now, however, it may be that I have done so in the struggle between Life and Death, between England and Germany, Liberty and Slavery. In any case, I shall have done my duty in my little way.

Well, Dad, please carry on with a good heart, then I shall be content.

Goodbye, dearest of fathers, goodbye E - - - and G - - - . May you all reap benefits of this great war and keep happy and cheery through life.

Your affectionate son and brother,

Glyn

Glyn Rhys Morgan was killed on 1st August 1917, two days after writing this letter. He was 21.

BEFORE ACTION

By all the glories of the day
And the cool evening's benison,
By that last sunset touch that lay
Upon the hills when day was done,
By beauty lavishly outpoured
And blessings carelessly received,
By all the days that I have lived
Make me a soldier, Lord.

By all of man's hopes and fears,
And all the wonders poets sing,
The laughter of unclouded years,
And every sad and lovely thing;
By the romantic ages stored
With high endeavour that was his,
By all his mad catastrophes
Make me a man, O Lord.

I, that on my familiar hill
Saw with uncomprehending eyes
A hundred of Thy sunsets spill
Their fresh and sanguine sacrifice,
Ere the sun swings his noonday sword
Must say goodbye to all of this; —
By all delights that I shall miss,
Help me to die, O Lord.

W.N. Hodgson

RENDEZVOUS[1]

I have a rendezvous with Death
At some disputed barricade,[2]
When Spring comes back with rustling shade
And apple-blossoms fill the air —
I have a rendezvous with Death
When Spring brings back blue days and fair.

It may be he shall take my hand
And lead me into his dark land
And close my eyes and quench my breath —
It may be I shall pass him[3] still.
I have a rendezvous with Death
On some scarred slope of battered hill,
When Spring comes round again this year
And the first meadow-flowers appear.

God knows 'twere better to be deep
Pillowed in silk and scented down,[4]
Where love throbs out in blissful sleep,
Pulse nigh to pulse, and breath to breath,
Where hushed awakenings are dear . . .
But I've a rendezvous with Death
At midnight in some flaming town,
When Spring trips north again this year,
And I to my pledged word[5] am true,
I shall not fail that rendezvous.

Alan Seeger

1 appointment   2 barrier, though, in fact, the front line trench or no-man's land that divided two
opposing armies   3 *pass him* - avoid dying   4 down-filled mattress or pillow   5 *pledged word* -
promise to fight for his country

NOON

It is midday: the deep trench glares . . .
A buzz and blaze of flies . . .
The hot wind puffs the giddy airs . . .
The great sun rakes the skies.

No sound in all the stagnant trench
Where forty standing men
Endure the sweat and grit and stench,
Like cattle in a pen.

Sometimes a sniper's[1] bullet whirs
Or twangs the whining wire
Sometimes a soldier sighs and stirs
As in hell's frying fire.

From out a high cool cloud descends
An aeroplane's far moan . . .
The sun strikes down, the thin cloud rends . . .
The black spot travels on.

And sweating, dizzied, isolate
In the hot trench beneath,
We bide[2] the next shrewd move of fate
Be it of life or death.

Robert Nichols

1 lone soldier with rifle firing at any member of enemy forces who might carelessly reveal himself
2 wait for

THE WOUNDED

Many millions of men were wounded in the war and no one knows the true figure. If one assumes that twice as many were injured as died there would have been 16 to 20 million wounded. Many, of course, recovered sufficiently from wounds to return to suffer again.

Wounded surviving in Britain

In Britain, by 1929 the Government had paid disability awards to 2.4 million men. For most of the men their suffering stayed with them and their families for the remainder of their lives.

Twenty years after the war had ended and large numbers of the wounded had died the Government was still paying disability pensions to the following numbers of men:

STILL SUFFERING FROM NEURASTHENIA (SHELL SHOCK)	25,000
HEAD INJURIES, MEN UNABLE TO WORK	15,000
PERMANENT DEAFNESS	11,000
PARTIAL BLINDNESS	8,000
TOTAL BLINDNESS	2,000
AMPUTATION OF ONE OR BOTH ARMS	3,600
WITHERED OR USELESS LIMB	90,000
ONE OR BOTH LEGS AMPUTATED	8,000
DISABILITY FROM FROSTBITE	2,200
EFFECTS OF GASSING	40,000

Casualties and politicians

Politicians were not isolated from the war and its suffering. Lloyd George's son and Asquith's four sons fought in the war. Herbert Asquith, the poet, was wounded four times and lost a leg below the knee. His brilliant brother, Raymond, was killed in the Battle of Loos.

The Prime Minister wrote of his son, Raymond, "Whatever pride I had in the past, and whatever hope I had for the future, by much the largest part was invested in him. Now all that is gone."

GAS ATTACKS

The first significant use of poison gas in war was on 22nd April 1915 when the Germans used it at Langemarck near Ypres, against French Algerian troops. During the First World War various types of gas were used – mustard, chlorine, phosgene, prussic acid and chloropicrin (tear gas). The effects of some of these gases were hideous.

Mustard gas blistered the skin, made the eyes extremely painful and caused vomiting. It burned into the bronchial tubes stripping off the mucous membrane. The pain was so intense that most mustard gas victims had to be strapped to their beds where their slow and agonising deaths lasted for up to five weeks.

Lance Sergeant Elmer Cotton describes the effects of **chlorine gas**:

> It produces a flooding in the lungs . . . a splitting headache, terrific thirst (to drink water is instant death), a knife edge pain in the lungs and the coughing up of a greenish froth off the stomach and lungs, ending finally in insensibility and death. The colour of the skin turns a greenish black and yellow, the tongue protrudes and the eyes assume a glassy stare.

Gas attacks became common

It is possible to gain the impression that gas was only occasionally used in the war, and that only the Germans used this hideous weapon. In fact one hundred and fifty thousand tons of gas were used in the war – most of it on the Western Front, and both sides used it. The main users of gas were Germany (68,000 tons), France (37,000 tons) and Britain (26,000 tons).

(Wilfred Owen's famous poem about a gas attack is on pages 160, 161.)

IN FLANDERS FIELDS

In Flanders fields the poppies blow
Between the crosses, row on row,
That mark our place; and in the sky
The larks, still bravely singing, fly
Scarce heard amid the guns below.

We are the Dead. Short days ago
We lived, felt dawn, saw sunset glow,
Loved and were loved, and now we lie
In Flanders fields.

Take up our quarrel with the foe:
To you from failing hands we throw
The torch; be yours to hold it high.
If ye break faith with us who die
We shall not sleep, though poppies grow
In Flanders fields.

John McCrae

In Flanders Fields was written near Ypres in May 1915, when McCrae, a Canadian doctor, was tending hundreds of mainly British gas victims. The poem was first published in *Punch*, on 8th December 1915.

THE SLAUGHTER

A low estimate of the First World War death toll suggests

Victors   The Allied Powers   – 5.1 million dead

Vanquished   The Central Powers – 3.5 million dead.

This amounted to an average of over five and a half thousand men killed every day of the war.

In the four years of The First World War three quarters of a million British men were killed.

THE SOMME

Every battle had its awful death toll. History's worst first day was the first day of the Battle of the Somme, on 1st July 1916. A hundred and ten thousand British men attacked the Germans that day. Twenty thousand British soldiers were killed and forty thousand were wounded.   – In the second week, British losses were running at ten thousand per day.

Confident that the massive shelling of the German lines over seven days had virtually wiped out the German army of the Somme and that success would therefore be a walkover, Field Marshal Haig, a devout Christian, wrote to his wife shortly before the battle, "I feel every step of the plan has been taken with Divine help."

In his diary, on 2nd of July, Haig wrote, "A day of downs and ups . . . The A G reported today that the total casualties are estimated at over 40,000 to date. This cannot be considered severe in view of the numbers engaged, and the length of front attacked."

(The way the British press reported the Somme campaign is illustrated on page 62.)

Somme casualties

The British and British Empire casualties for the Battle of the Somme amounted to 420,000 men. The French lost 200,000 men. The Germans an uncertain number. Estimates range between 210,000 and 650,000.

...ite ward I stand,
...athless space,
... fevered hand,
...t's commonplace[1] —

... to feel the cold
...ut my heart;
...uncontrolled,
...f pity start.

... as best I may,
...rs of pain to ease,
... – *Far away*
...*en as these?*

...l

...RD?

...ife, boy,
... limb:
...e his precious wits,
...d for him?

...ry,
...is rest.
... poor babbler here
...on his breast?

...e,
...used and dim,
... a sacrifice
...d for him?

...ts

...First World War apart from the daily
...that over the whole of Europe espe-
...rld too, there was a sense that a whole
...r ten million men; and many survivors
...y.

The battle had been intended to make rapid progress through the German lines. When it ended after five months of bloodshed, the British and Empire forces had advanced about six miles and were still three miles short of Bapaume which had been one of the first day's objectives.

Winston Churchill's view

I view with the utmost pain, the terrible and disproportionate slaughter of our troops. We have not conquered in a month's fighting as much ground as we were expected to gain in the first two hours.

Memorandum, August, 1916

Lloyd George's considered opinion

The wasteful prolongation of the Somme campaign after it had become clear that a break through the German lines was unattainable was a case where the Government might have intervened. It cost us heavily. The volunteers of 1914 and 1915 were the finest body of men ever sent to do battle for Britain. Five hundred thousand of these men, the flower of our race, were thrown away on a stubborn and unintelligent hammering away at what was then an impenetrable barrier.

THE STRESS OF WAR

The horrors and shocks of front line experience were too much for many soldiers. Field Marshal Haig coped with this problem by shutting it out. For the Battle of the Somme he placed his headquarters well away from the scene of the main fighting and stayed there. He soon learned to avoid the distress of visiting wounded soldiers in casualty clearing stations because he found that such visits made him physically sick.

All front line soldiers who survived were deeply affected by their experiences for the rest of their lives. Many were temporarily or permanently tipped into madness. Within ten years of the end of the war 114,000 men had applied for pensions on the grounds of mental disabilities.

At first the condition of shell-shock and mental breakdown was not accepted as an illness and it was not until 1917 that special centres were set up on the Western Front to deal with severe cases of mental distress. Many men, after a period of rest and quiet, were able to return to the trenches. Others never recovered.

In Britain, in addition to six peacetime hospitals that could deal with nervous disorders an additional six hospitals for officers and

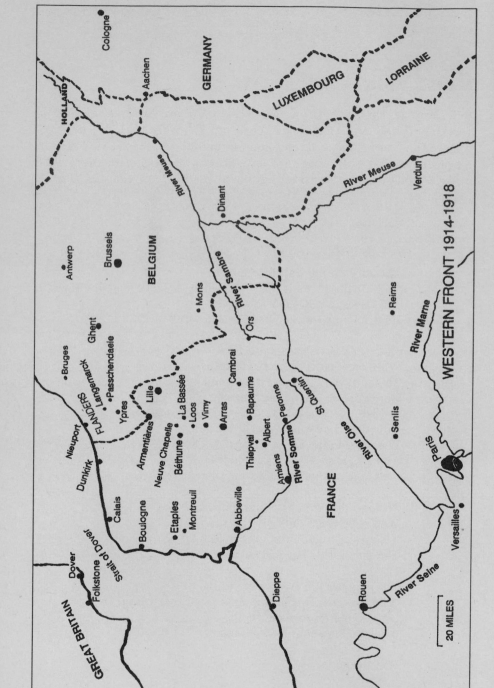

Cologne

GERMANY

LUXEMBOURG

LORRAINE

HOLLAND

Aachen

River Meuse

River Meuse

Verdun

Dinant

Brussels

Antwerp

BELGIUM

River Sambre

Mons

WESTERN FRONT 1914-1918

Reims

River Marne

Ors

Ghent

Bruges

Langemarck

Passchendaele

FLANDERS

Ypres

Lille

Cambrai

Bapaume

Peronne

St Quentin

Senlis

Nieuport

Armentières

Neuve Chapelle

La Bassée

Loos

Vimy

Arras

Albert

Thiepval

River Oise

Paris

Dunkirk

Béthune

Amiens

River Somme

Calais

Boulogne

Etaples

Montreuil

Abbeville

FRANCE

Versailles

GREAT BRITAIN

Dover

Folkstone

Strait of Dover

Dieppe

Rouen

River Seine

20 MILES

THE NURSE

Here in the long w
Pausing a little bre
Touching a restles
Murmuring comfo

Long enough pause
Fingers of fear abo
Just for a moment,
All the pent tears o

While here I strive
Strangers' long hou
Dumbly I question
Lies my beloved e

Miss G M Mitchel

1 common words of comfort

WHAT REWA

You gave your l
And *you* gave a
But he who gav
Say, what rewar

One has his glo
One has found l
But what of this
With chin sunk

Flotsam of battl
With brain bem
O God, for such
Say, what rewar

Winifred M. Le

BEREAVEMENT

What sets the bereavement of the
tragedies of a peacetime world is
cially, but in other parts of the wo
generation had been lost – nine o
searched in vain for the reason w

In Britain 160,000 women lost their husbands, and 300,000 children lost their fathers.

The literature generated by this tragedy is colossal. The mourning commemorated in war memorials throughout Europe and around the world shows the extraordinary scale and importance of the trauma inflicted by the First World War.

THE WIND ON THE DOWNS[1]

I like to think of you as brown and tall,
As strong and living as you used to be,
In khaki tunic, Sam Brown belt[2] and all,
And standing there and laughing down at me,
Because they tell me, dear, that you are dead,
Because I can no longer see your face.
You have not died, it is not true, instead
You seek adventure in some other place.
That you are round about me, I believe;
I hear you laughing as you used to do,
Yet loving all the things I think of you;
And knowing you are happy, should I grieve?
You follow and are watchful where I go;
How should you leave me, having loved me so?

We walked along the tow-path, you and I,
Beside the sluggish-moving, still canal;
It seemed impossible that you should die;
I think of you the same and always shall.
We thought of many things and spoke of few,
And life lay all uncertainly before,
And now I walk alone and think of you,
And wonder what new kingdoms you explore.
Over the railway line, across the grass,
While up above the golden wings are spread,
Flying, ever flying overhead,
Here still I see your khaki figure pass,
And when I leave the meadow, almost wait
That you should open first the wooden gate.

Marian Allen

1 lines of hills in southern England   2 *Sam Brown belt* - army belt with strap passing over right shoulder

THE MOTHER

If you should die, think only this of me
In that still quietness where is space for thought,
Where parting, loss and bloodshed shall not be,
And men may rest themselves and dream of nought:
That in some place a mystic mile away
One whom you loved has drained the bitter cup[1]
Till there is nought to drink; has faced the day
Once more, and now, has raised the standard[2] up.

And think, my son, with eyes grown clear and dry
She lives as though for ever in your sight,
Loving the things you loved, with heart aglow
For country, honour, truth, traditions high, –
Proud that you paid their price.[3] (And if some night
Her heart should break –   well, lad, you will not know.)

May Herschel-Clarke, first published 1917

1 *bitter cup* - the cup of life 2 *raised the standard* - rallied to the flag, supported the country's
cause 3 *paid their price* - died for their country as required by political and military leaders

Repression of feelings

Millions daily feared news of the death of a soldier close to them.
Apart from her fiancé, Roland Leighton, Vera Brittain had lost other
friends, killed in action. When, on June 16th, 1918, she read news of
heavy fighting in Italy where her brother was stationed, she feared the
worst. Of that time she wrote, "There was nothing to do in the midst of
one's family but practise that concealment of fear which the long years
of war had instilled, thrusting it inward until one's subconscious became
a regular prison-house of apprehensions and inhibitions which were
later to take their revenge." (*Testament of Youth*.)

Some days later she received news of her brother's death. She wrote,

> There came the sudden loud clattering at the front-door knocker
> that always meant a telegram.
>
> For a moment I thought that my legs would not carry me, but they
> behaved quite normally as I got up and went to the door. I knew
> what was in the telegram – I had known for a week   – but
> because the persistent hopefulness of the human heart refuses to
> allow intuitive certainty to persuade the reason of that which it
> knows, I opened and read it in a tearing anguish of suspense.
>
> "Regret to inform you Captain E H Brittain, MC, killed in action
> Italy June 15th."

"No answer," I told the boy mechanically, and handed the telegram to my father, who had followed me into the hall. As we went back into the dining-room I saw, as though I had never seen them before, the bowl of blue delphiniums on the table; their intense colour, vivid, ethereal, seemed too radiant for earthly flowers.

Long after the family had gone to bed and the world had grown silent, I crept into the dining-room to be alone with Edward's portrait. Carefully closing the door, I turned on the light and looked at the pale, pictured face, so dignified, so steadfast, so tragically mature. He had been through so much – far, far more than those beloved friends who had died at an earlier stage of the interminable War, leaving him alone to mourn their loss. Fate might have allowed him the little, sorry compensation of survival, the chance to make his lovely music in honour of their memory. It seemed indeed the last irony that he should have been killed by the countrymen of Fritz Kreisler, the violinist whom of all others he had most greatly admired.

And suddenly, as I remembered all the dear afternoons and evenings when I had followed him on the piano as he played his violin, the sad, searching eyes of the portrait were more than I could bear, and falling on my knees before it I began to cry "Edward! Oh, Edward!" in dazed repetition, as though my persistent crying and calling would somehow bring him back.

PRAEMATURI[1]

When men are old, and their friends die,
They are not so sad,
Because their love is running slow,
And cannot spring from the wound with so sharp a pain;
And they are happy with many memories,
And only a little while to be alone.

But we are young, and our friends are dead
Suddenly, and our quick love is torn in two;
So our memories are only hopes that came to nothing.
We are left alone like old men; we should be dead –
But there are years and years in which we shall still be young.

Margaret Postgate Cole

1 premature death

11

SIEGFRIED SASSOON 1886-1967

EARLY ATTITUDES TO THE WAR

Siegfried Sassoon, who was to become very bitter about the war as time went on, was the first of the well-known war poets to sign up in response to the actions of Germany. He had his medical inspection on 1st August 1914, and was in uniform the day after Britain declared war on Germany. Why he was so quick to join up is not clear. In his *Memoirs of a Fox-hunting Man* he gives us a few clues.

> The war was inevitable and justifiable. Courage remained a virtue . . . I had serious aspirations to heroism . . . My one idea was to be first in the field. In fact I made quite an impressive inward emotional experience of it. . . My gesture was, so to speak, an individual one, and I gloried in it.

He was, however, thinking seriously about what the war meant. His first war poems, not surprisingly, are in keeping with the popular spirit of the times. His bitterness and hatred of the war did not begin until early 1916.

ABSOLUTION[1]

The anguish of the earth absolves[2] our eyes
Till beauty shines in all that we can see.
War is our scourge; yet war has made us wise,
And, fighting for our freedom, we are free.

Horror of wounds and anger at the foe,
And loss of things desired; all these must pass.
We are the happy legion, for we know
Time's but a golden wind that shakes the grass.

There was an hour when we were loth[3] to part
From life we longed to share no less than others.
Now, having claimed this heritage of heart,
What need we more, my comrades and my brothers?

April-September, 1915

1 release from guilt or blame   2 takes the guilt away   3 reluctant, unwilling

Extracts from Siegfried Sassoon's Diary – attitudes to killing and death

March 31st 1916

No good being out here unless one takes the full amount of risks, and I want to get a good name in the Battalion, for the sake of poetry and poets, whom I represent.

April 1st 1916

I used to say I couldn't kill anyone in this war; but, since they shot Tommy, I would gladly stick a bayonet into a German by daylight.

PEACE

Down glaring dusty roads, a sanctuary of trees,
Green for my gaze and cool, and hushed with pigeon's croon:
Chill pitcher'd water for my thirst; and sweet as these,
Anger grown tired of hate, and peace returning soon.

In my heart there's cruel war that must be waged
In darkness vile with moans and bleeding bodies maimed;
A gnawing hunger drives me, wild to be assuaged,
And bitter lust chuckles within me unashamed.

Come back to heal me when my feckless[1] course is run,
Peace, that I sought in life; crown me among the dead;
Stoop to me like a lover when the fight is done;
Fold me in sleep; and let the stars be overhead.

2 April, 1916

1 useless

Diary entry, April 4th 1916

I want to smash someone's skull; I want to have a scrap and get out of the war for a bit or for ever. Sitting in a trench waiting for a rifle-grenade isn't fighting: war is clambering out of the top trench at 3 o'clock in the morning with a lot of rum-drugged soldiers who don't know where they're going – half of them to be blasted with machine-guns at point-blank range – trying to get over the wire which our artillery have failed to destroy. I can't get my own back for Hamo and Tommy that way. While I am really

angry with the enemy, as I am lately, I must work it off, as these
things don't last long with me as a rule. If I get shot it will be
rotten for some people at home, but I am bound to get it in the
neck sometime, so why not make a creditable show, and let people
see that poets can fight as well as anybody else? And death is the
best adventure of all – better than living idleness and sinking into
the groove again and trying to be happy. Life is precious to us all
now; too precious to keep long.

THE POET AS HERO

You've heard me, scornful, harsh, and discontented,
Mocking and loathing War: you've asked me why
Of my old, silly sweetness I've repented –
My ecstasies changed to an ugly cry.

You are aware that once I sought the Grail,[1]
Riding in armour bright, serene and strong;
And it was told that through my infant wail
There rose immortal semblances of song.

But now I've said good-bye to Galahad,[2]
And am no more the knight of dreams and show:
For lust and senseless hatred make me glad,
And my killed friends are with me where I go.
Wound for red wound I burn to smite their wrongs;
And there is absolution[3] in my songs.

1916

1 Holy Grail, a bowl, said to have been used by Jesus and brought to England by Joseph of
Arimathea. It was lost and medieval knights are said to have gone in search of it. Sassoon
imagined himself as a knight in medieval armour 2 the most virtuous of the legendary knights of
King Arthur 3 release from feelings of guilt

A NIGHT ATTACK

The rank stench of those bodies haunts me still,
And I remember things I'd best forget,
For now we've marched to a green, trenchless land
Twelve miles from battering guns: along the grass
Brown lines of tents are hives for snoring men;
Wide, radiant water sways the floating sky
Below dark, shivering trees. And living-clean
Comes back with thoughts of home and hours of sleep.

The battle had been intended to make rapid progress through the German lines. When it ended after five months of bloodshed, the British and Empire forces had advanced about six miles and were still three miles short of Bapaume which had been one of the first day's objectives.

Winston Churchill's view

I view with the utmost pain, the terrible and disproportionate slaughter of our troops. We have not conquered in a month's fighting as much ground as we were expected to gain in the first two hours.

Memorandum, August, 1916

Lloyd George's considered opinion

The wasteful prolongation of the Somme campaign after it had become clear that a break through the German lines was unattainable was a case where the Government might have intervened. It cost us heavily. The volunteers of 1914 and 1915 were the finest body of men ever sent to do battle for Britain. Five hundred thousand of these men, the flower of our race, were thrown away on a stubborn and unintelligent hammering away at what was then an impenetrable barrier.

THE STRESS OF WAR

The horrors and shocks of front line experience were too much for many soldiers. Field Marshal Haig coped with this problem by shutting it out. For the Battle of the Somme he placed his headquarters well away from the scene of the main fighting and stayed there. He soon learned to avoid the distress of visiting wounded soldiers in casualty clearing stations because he found that such visits made him physically sick.

All front line soldiers who survived were deeply affected by their experiences for the rest of their lives. Many were temporarily or permanently tipped into madness. Within ten years of the end of the war 114,000 men had applied for pensions on the grounds of mental disabilities.

At first the condition of shell-shock and mental breakdown was not accepted as an illness and it was not until 1917 that special centres were set up on the Western Front to deal with severe cases of mental distress. Many men, after a period of rest and quiet, were able to return to the trenches. Others never recovered.

In Britain, in addition to six peacetime hospitals that could deal with nervous disorders an additional six hospitals for officers and

thirteen for other ranks were set up in 1917 and 1918 to deal
entirely with those whose mental balance had been
disturbed by their experiences in the trenches, and who had been
sent home for ever.

Martin Gilbert, *First World War*, p358

The Medical History of the War estimated that about 2 per cent of sol-
diers suffered from shell-shock – about 80,000 men driven temporar-
ily or permanently insane.

Even those who would still be regarded as "normal" often changed their
personalities. Vera Brittain noted that her brother Edward who was
home on leave had changed. He had become, "unfamiliar, frightening
Edward, who never smiled or spoke except about trivial things, who
seemed to have nothing to say to me and indeed hardly appeared to no-
tice my return."

Being shown the mad ward

Jeffrey Farnol was once being shown round a Base Hospital when they
came across what the doctor called the "mad ward". Farnol described
a room full of men with "a vagueness of gaze, a loose-lipped, too-
ready smile, a vacancy of expression. Some there were who
scowled sullenly enough, others who crouched apart, solitary souls,
who, I learned, felt themselves outcasts: others who crouched in
corners haunted by the dread of pursuing vengeance always at hand."

Philip Gibbs saw similar cases – such as the sergeant-major in Aveluy
Wood, near Thiepval, who was "convulsed with a dreadful rigor like
a man in epilepsy, and clawed at his mouth, moaning horribly, with blind
terror in his eyes. He had to be strapped to a stretcher before he could
be carried away."

In almost the same place he saw a Wiltshire boy standing outside a
dugout; "shaking in every limb, in a palsied way. His steel hat was at
the back of his head, and his mouth slobbered, and two comrades could
not hold him still. These badly shell-shocked boys clawed at their
mouths ceaselessly. It was a common dreadful action. Others sat in
field hospitals in a state of coma, dazed, as though deaf, and actu-
ally dumb."

Deserters

Some men coped with stress by trying to run away. If caught they were
tried by court martial and if found guilty were usually shot. According
to official statistics 112 British soldiers were shot for desertion. It is
believed that some were unofficially shot by their officers. A powerful

scene in R C Sherriff's play, *Journey's End* shows how a would-be deserter might have been dealt with.

MORAL CONFLICT

R E Vernède, having been wounded in 1916 was offered a safe job working in the War Office, but believed so strongly in the need to oppose the Germans that he insisted on returning to the front line. For Vernède, whilst believing in the rightness of his cause, there was bewilderment at the contrast between his actions and his moral principles.

A LISTENING POST

The sun's a red ball in the oak
And all the grass is grey with dew,
A while ago a blackbird spoke –
He didn't know the world's askew.[1]

And yonder rifleman and I
Wait here behind the misty trees
To shoot the first man that goes by,
Our rifles ready on our knees.

How could he know that if we fail
The world may lie in chains[2] for years
And England be a bygone tale
And right be wrong, and laughter tears?

Strange that this bird sits there and sings
While we must only sit and plan –
Who are so much the higher things –
The murder of our fellow man . . .

But maybe God will cause to be –
Who brought forth sweetness from the strong[3] –
Out of our discords harmony
Sweeter than that bird's song.

R E Vernède, 1917

1 twisted, in a mess   2 *world may lie in chains* - countries may come under German control   3 *sweetness from the strong* - reference to the Bible story (Judges, chapter 14) of honey made by bees in the body of a dead lion.

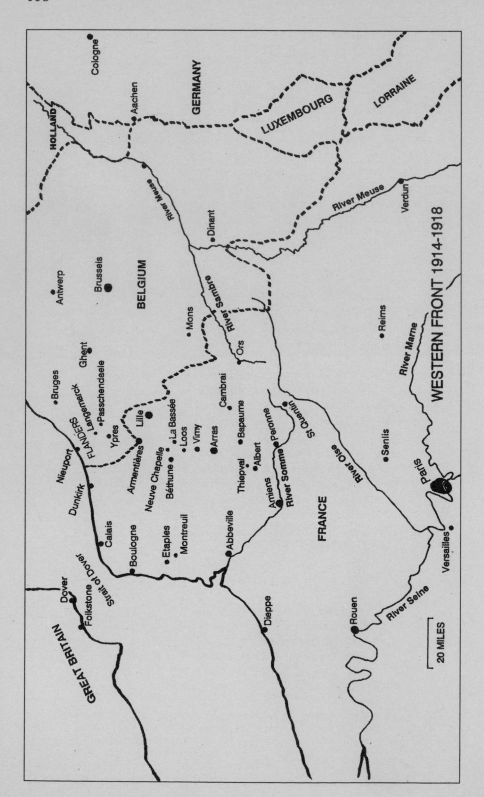

WESTERN FRONT 1914-1918

10

WOMEN POETS - PART TWO

THE WOUNDED RETURN

Throughout the war British soldiers with serious wounds were returned
by boat and train to England to be treated. Many returned to fight again;
others became permanently disabled, or died. Peacetime hospitals were
soon overwhelmed by the numbers of wounded arriving and hundreds
of existing buildings were converted for use as hospitals, including
schools and the palace built by George IV, the *Royal Pavilion* in Brighton.
Large numbers of women volunteered to work in these new hospitals.

PLUCK

Crippled for life at seventeen,
His great eyes seem to question why:
With both legs smashed it might have been
Better in that grim trench to die
Than drag maimed years out helplessly.

A child — so wasted and so white,
He told a lie[1] to get his way,
To march, a man with men, and fight
While other boys are still at play.
A gallant lie your heart will say.

So broke with pain, he shrinks in dread
To see the "dresser" drawing near;
And winds the clothes about his head
That none may see his heart-sick fear.
His shaking, strangled sobs you hear.

But when the dreaded moment's there
He'll face us all, a soldier yet,
Watch his bared wounds with unmoved air,
(Though tell-tale lashes still are wet),
And smoke his Woodbine cigarette.

Eva Dobell

1 claimed he was older than he was to get into the fighting

THE NURSE

Here in the long white ward I stand,
Pausing a little breathless space,
Touching a restless fevered hand,
Murmuring comfort's commonplace[1] –

Long enough pause to feel the cold
Fingers of fear about my heart;
Just for a moment, uncontrolled,
All the pent tears of pity start.

While here I strive as best I may,
Strangers' long hours of pain to ease,
Dumbly I question – *Far away
Lies my beloved even as these?*

Miss G M Mitchell

1 common words of comfort

WHAT REWARD?

You gave your life, boy,
And *you* gave a limb:
But he who gave his precious wits,
Say, what reward for him?

One has his glory,
One has found his rest.
But what of this poor babbler here
With chin sunk on his breast?

Flotsam of battle,
With brain bemused and dim,
O God, for such a sacrifice
Say, what reward for him?

Winifred M. Letts

BEREAVEMENT

What sets the bereavement of the First World War apart from the daily tragedies of a peacetime world is that over the whole of Europe especially, but in other parts of the world too, there was a sense that a whole generation had been lost – nine or ten million men; and many survivors searched in vain for the reason why.

In Britain 160,000 women lost their husbands, and 300,000 children lost their fathers.

The literature generated by this tragedy is colossal. The mourning commemorated in war memorials throughout Europe and around the world shows the extraordinary scale and importance of the trauma inflicted by the First World War.

THE WIND ON THE DOWNS[1]

I like to think of you as brown and tall,
As strong and living as you used to be,
In khaki tunic, Sam Brown belt[2] and all,
And standing there and laughing down at me,
Because they tell me, dear, that you are dead,
Because I can no longer see your face.
You have not died, it is not true, instead
You seek adventure in some other place.
That you are round about me, I believe;
I hear you laughing as you used to do,
Yet loving all the things I think of you;
And knowing you are happy, should I grieve?
You follow and are watchful where I go;
How should you leave me, having loved me so?

We walked along the tow-path, you and I,
Beside the sluggish-moving, still canal;
It seemed impossible that you should die;
I think of you the same and always shall.
We thought of many things and spoke of few,
And life lay all uncertainly before,
And now I walk alone and think of you,
And wonder what new kingdoms you explore.
Over the railway line, across the grass,
While up above the golden wings are spread,
Flying, ever flying overhead,
Here still I see your khaki figure pass,
And when I leave the meadow, almost wait
That you should open first the wooden gate.

Marian Allen

1 lines of hills in southern England   2 *Sam Brown belt* - army belt with strap passing over right shoulder

THE MOTHER

If you should die, think only this of me
In that still quietness where is space for thought,
Where parting, loss and bloodshed shall not be,
And men may rest themselves and dream of nought:
That in some place a mystic mile away
One whom you loved has drained the bitter cup[1]
Till there is nought to drink; has faced the day
Once more, and now, has raised the standard[2] up.

And think, my son, with eyes grown clear and dry
She lives as though for ever in your sight,
Loving the things you loved, with heart aglow
For country, honour, truth, traditions high, –
Proud that you paid their price.[3] (And if some night
Her heart should break – well, lad, you will not know.)

May Herschel-Clarke, first published 1917

1 *bitter cup* - the cup of life 2 *raised the standard* - rallied to the flag, supported the country's
cause 3 *paid their price* - died for their country as required by political and military leaders

Repression of feelings

Millions daily feared news of the death of a soldier close to them.
Apart from her fiancé, Roland Leighton, Vera Brittain had lost other
friends, killed in action. When, on June 16th, 1918, she read news of
heavy fighting in Italy where her brother was stationed, she feared the
worst. Of that time she wrote, "There was nothing to do in the midst of
one's family but practise that concealment of fear which the long years
of war had instilled, thrusting it inward until one's subconscious became
a regular prison-house of apprehensions and inhibitions which were
later to take their revenge." (*Testament of Youth*.)

Some days later she received news of her brother's death. She wrote,

> There came the sudden loud clattering at the front-door knocker
> that always meant a telegram.

> For a moment I thought that my legs would not carry me, but they
> behaved quite normally as I got up and went to the door. I knew
> what was in the telegram – I had known for a week   – but
> because the persistent hopefulness of the human heart refuses to
> allow intuitive certainty to persuade the reason of that which it
> knows, I opened and read it in a tearing anguish of suspense.

> "Regret to inform you Captain E H Brittain, MC, killed in action
> Italy June 15th."

"No answer," I told the boy mechanically, and handed the telegram to my father, who had followed me into the hall. As we went back into the dining-room I saw, as though I had never seen them before, the bowl of blue delphiniums on the table; their intense colour, vivid, ethereal, seemed too radiant for earthly flowers.

Long after the family had gone to bed and the world had grown silent, I crept into the dining-room to be alone with Edward's portrait. Carefully closing the door, I turned on the light and looked at the pale, pictured face, so dignified, so steadfast, so tragically mature. He had been through so much − far, far more than those beloved friends who had died at an earlier stage of the interminable War, leaving him alone to mourn their loss. Fate might have allowed him the little, sorry compensation of survival, the chance to make his lovely music in honour of their memory. It seemed indeed the last irony that he should have been killed by the countrymen of Fritz Kreisler, the violinist whom of all others he had most greatly admired.

And suddenly, as I remembered all the dear afternoons and evenings when I had followed him on the piano as he played his violin, the sad, searching eyes of the portrait were more than I could bear, and falling on my knees before it I began to cry "Edward! Oh, Edward!" in dazed repetition, as though my persistent crying and calling would somehow bring him back.

PRAEMATURI[1]

When men are old, and their friends die,
They are not so sad,
Because their love is running slow,
And cannot spring from the wound with so sharp a pain;
And they are happy with many memories,
And only a little while to be alone.

But we are young, and our friends are dead
Suddenly, and our quick love is torn in two;
So our memories are only hopes that came to nothing.
We are left alone like old men; we should be dead −
But there are years and years in which we shall still be young.

Margaret Postgate Cole

1 premature death

11

SIEGFRIED SASSOON 1886-1967

EARLY ATTITUDES TO THE WAR

Siegfried Sassoon, who was to become very bitter about the war as time went on, was the first of the well-known war poets to sign up in response to the actions of Germany. He had his medical inspection on 1st August 1914, and was in uniform the day after Britain declared war on Germany. Why he was so quick to join up is not clear. In his *Memoirs of a Fox-hunting Man* he gives us a few clues.

> The war was inevitable and justifiable. Courage remained a virtue . . . I had serious aspirations to heroism . . . My one idea was to be first in the field. In fact I made quite an impressive inward emotional experience of it. . . My gesture was, so to speak, an individual one, and I gloried in it.

He was, however, thinking seriously about what the war meant. His first war poems, not surprisingly, are in keeping with the popular spirit of the times. His bitterness and hatred of the war did not begin until early 1916.

ABSOLUTION[1]

The anguish of the earth absolves[2] our eyes
Till beauty shines in all that we can see.
War is our scourge; yet war has made us wise,
And, fighting for our freedom, we are free.

Horror of wounds and anger at the foe,
And loss of things desired; all these must pass.
We are the happy legion, for we know
Time's but a golden wind that shakes the grass.

There was an hour when we were loth[3] to part
From life we longed to share no less than others.
Now, having claimed this heritage of heart,
What need we more, my comrades and my brothers?

April-September, 1915

1 release from guilt or blame   2 takes the guilt away   3 reluctant, unwilling

Extracts from Siegfried Sassoon's Diary – attitudes to killing and death

March 31st 1916

No good being out here unless one takes the full amount of risks, and I want to get a good name in the Battalion, for the sake of poetry and poets, whom I represent.

April 1st 1916

I used to say I couldn't kill anyone in this war; but, since they shot Tommy, I would gladly stick a bayonet into a German by daylight.

PEACE

Down glaring dusty roads, a sanctuary of trees,
Green for my gaze and cool, and hushed with pigeon's croon:
Chill pitcher'd water for my thirst; and sweet as these,
Anger grown tired of hate, and peace returning soon.

In my heart there's cruel war that must be waged
In darkness vile with moans and bleeding bodies maimed;
A gnawing hunger drives me, wild to be assuaged,
And bitter lust chuckles within me unashamed.

Come back to heal me when my feckless[1] course is run,
Peace, that I sought in life; crown me among the dead;
Stoop to me like a lover when the fight is done;
Fold me in sleep; and let the stars be overhead.

2 April, 1916

1 useless

Diary entry, April 4th 1916

I want to smash someone's skull; I want to have a scrap and get out of the war for a bit or for ever. Sitting in a trench waiting for a rifle-grenade isn't fighting: war is clambering out of the top trench at 3 o'clock in the morning with a lot of rum-drugged soldiers who don't know where they're going – half of them to be blasted with machine-guns at point-blank range – trying to get over the wire which our artillery have failed to destroy. I can't get my own back for Hamo and Tommy that way. While I am really

angry with the enemy, as I am lately, I must work it off, as these
things don't last long with me as a rule. If I get shot it will be
rotten for some people at home, but I am bound to get it in the
neck sometime, so why not make a creditable show, and let people
see that poets can fight as well as anybody else? And death is the
best adventure of all — better than living idleness and sinking into
the groove again and trying to be happy. Life is precious to us all
now; too precious to keep long.

THE POET AS HERO

You've heard me, scornful, harsh, and discontented,
Mocking and loathing War: you've asked me why
Of my old, silly sweetness I've repented —
My ecstasies changed to an ugly cry.

You are aware that once I sought the Grail,[1]
Riding in armour bright, serene and strong;
And it was told that through my infant wail
There rose immortal semblances of song.

But now I've said good-bye to Galahad,[2]
And am no more the knight of dreams and show:
For lust and senseless hatred make me glad,
And my killed friends are with me where I go.
Wound for red wound I burn to smite their wrongs;
And there is absolution[3] in my songs.

1916

1 Holy Grail, a bowl, said to have been used by Jesus and brought to England by Joseph of
Arimathea. It was lost and medieval knights are said to have gone in search of it. Sassoon
imagined himself as a knight in medieval armour 2 the most virtuous of the legendary knights of
King Arthur 3 release from feelings of guilt

A NIGHT ATTACK

The rank stench of those bodies haunts me still,
And I remember things I'd best forget,
For now we've marched to a green, trenchless land
Twelve miles from battering guns: along the grass
Brown lines of tents are hives for snoring men;
Wide, radiant water sways the floating sky
Below dark, shivering trees. And living-clean
Comes back with thoughts of home and hours of sleep.

Tonight I smell the battle; miles away
Gun-thunder leaps and thuds along the ridge;
The spouting shells dig pits in fields of death,
And wounded men are moaning in the woods.
If any friend be there whom I have loved,
God speed him safe to England with a gash.

It's sundown in the camp; some youngster laughs,
Lifting his mug and drinking health to all
Who come unscathed[1] from that unpitying waste.
(Terror and ruin lurk behind his gaze.)
Another sits with tranquil, musing face,
Puffing his pipe and dreaming of the girl
Whose last scrawled letter lies upon his knee.
The sunlight falls, low-ruddy from the west,
Upon their heads; last week they might have died;
And now they stretch their limbs in tired content.

One says "The bloody Bosche[2] has got the knock;
And soon they'll crumple up and chuck their games.
We've got the beggars on the run at last!"
Then I remembered someone that I'd seen
Dead in a squalid, miserable ditch,
Heedless of toiling feet that trod him down.
He was a Prussian[3] with a decent face,
Young, fresh, and pleasant, so I dare to say.
No doubt he loathed the war and longed for peace,
And cursed our souls because we'd killed his friends.

One night he yawned along a half-dug trench
Midnight; and then the British guns began
With heavy shrapnel bursting low, and "hows"[4]
Whistling to cut the wire with blinding din.
He didn't move; the digging still went on;
Men stooped and shovelled; someone gave a grunt,
And moaned and died with agony in the sludge.
Then the long hiss of shells lifted and stopped.

He stared into the gloom; a rocket curved,
And rifles rattled angrily on the left
Down by the wood, and there was noise of bombs.
Then the damned English loomed in scrambling haste
Out of the dark and struggled through the wire,
And there were shouts and curses; someone screamed
And men began to blunder down the trench
Without their rifles. It was time to go:
He grabbed his coat; stood up, gulping some bread;
Then clutched his head and fell.

I found him there
In the gray morning when the place was held.
His face was in the mud; one arm flung out
As when he crumpled up; his sturdy legs
Were bent beneath his trunk; heels to the sky.

July, 1916

1 unharmed 2 Germans 3 German 4 howitzers, big field guns

THE HERO

"Jack fell as he'd have wished," the Mother said,
And folded up the letter that she'd read.
"The Colonel writes so nicely." Something broke
In the tired voice that quavered to a choke.
She half looked up. "We mothers are so proud
Of our dead soldiers." Then her face was bowed.

Quietly the Brother Officer went out.
He'd told the poor old dear some gallant[1] lies
That she would nourish[2] all her days, no doubt.
For while he coughed and mumbled, her weak eyes
Had shone with gentle triumph, brimmed with joy,
Because he'd been so brave, her glorious boy.

He thought how "Jack," cold-footed, useless swine,
Had panicked down the trench that night the mine
Went up at Wicked Corner; how he'd tried
To get sent home, and how, at last, he died,
Blown to small bits. And no one seemed to care
Except that lonely woman with white hair.

August, 1916

1 fine-sounding   2 be comforted by

SASSOON'S INTEREST IN RELIGION

Sassoon regarded himself as a religious poet as well as a war poet. Sometimes his interest in religion took the form of a religious longing; at other times he was bitterly critical of religious leaders during the war.

A MYSTIC AS SOLDIER

I lived my days apart,
Dreaming fair songs for God;
By the glory in my heart
Covered and crowned and shod.[1]

Now God is in the strife,
And I must seek Him there,
Where death outnumbers life,
And fury smites the air.

I walk the secret way
With anger in my brain.
O music through my clay,[2]
When will you sound again?

November, 1916

1 *Covered and crowned and shod* - his whole being shone with religious feelings   2 body

IN THE CHURCH OF ST OUEN

Time makes me be a soldier. But I know
That had I lived six hundred years ago
I might have tried to build within my heart
A church like this, where I could dwell apart
With chanting peace. My spirit longs for prayer;
And, lost to God, I seek him everywhere.

Here, where the windows burn and bloom like flowers,
And sunlight falls and fades with tranquil hours,
I could be half a saint, for like a rose
In heart-shaped stone the glory of Heaven glows.
But where I stand, desiring yet to stay,
Hearing rich music at the close of day,
The Spring Offensive[1] (Easter is its date)
Calls me. And that's the music I await.

At Rouen, 4 March, 1917

1 a large-scale attack

SOLDIERS

BASE DETAILS

If I were fierce, and bald, and short of breath,
I'd live with scarlet Majors at the Base,
And speed glum heroes up the line to death.
You'd see me with my puffy, petulant face,
Guzzling and gulping in the best hotel,
Reading the Roll of Honour. "Poor young chap,"
I'd say - "I used to know his father well;
Yes, we've lost heavily in this last scrap."
And when the war is done and youth stone dead,
I'd toddle safely home and die - in bed.

4 March, 1917

THE REAR-GUARD[1]
(Hindenburg Line[2] April 1917)

Groping along the tunnel, step by step,
He winked his prying torch with patching glare
From side to side, and sniffed the unwholesome air.

Tins, boxes, bottles, shapes too vague to know;
A mirror smashed, the mattress from a bed;
And he, exploring fifty feet below
The rosy gloom of battle overhead.

Tripping, he grabbed the wall; saw some one lie
Humped at his feet, half-hidden by a rug,
And stooped to give the sleeper's arm a tug.
"I'm looking for headquarters." No reply.

"God blast your neck!" (For days he'd had no sleep.)
"Get up and guide me through this stinking place."
Savage, he kicked a soft unanswering heap,
And flashed his beam across the livid face
Terribly glaring up, whose eyes yet wore
Agony dying hard ten days before;
And fists of fingers clutched a blackening wound.

Alone he staggered on until he found
Dawn's ghost that filtered down a shafted stair
To the dazed, muttering creatures underground
Who hear the boom of shells in muffled sound.
At last, with sweat of horror in his hair,
He climbed through darkness to the twilight air,
Unloading hell behind him step by step.

22 April, 1917

1 This poem has similarities to Owen's *Strange Meeting*   2 a long German line of trenches defended with deep concrete bunkers

THE GENERAL

"Good-morning, good morning!" the General[1] said
When we met him last week on our way to the line.
Now the soldiers he smiled at are most of 'em dead,
And we're cursing his staff for incompetent swine.
"He's a cheery old card," grunted Harry to Jack
As they slogged up to Arras with rifle and pack.

But he did for them both by his plan of attack.

Denmark Hill Hospital, April, 1917

1 *the General* - Sassoon may have been thinking of General Haig who had overall command of the British armies in France for most of the war

TO ANY DEAD OFFICER

Well, how are things in Heaven? I wish you'd say,
Because I'd like to know that you're all right.
Tell me, have you found everlasting day,
Or been sucked in by everlasting night?
For when I shut my eyes your face shows plain;
I hear you make some cheery old remark –
I can rebuild you in my brain,
Though you've gone out patrolling in the dark.

You hated tours of trenches; you were proud
Of nothing more than having good years to spend;
Longed to get home and join the careless crowd
Of chaps who work in peace with Time for friend.
That's all washed out now. You're beyond the wire:
No earthly chance can send you crawling back;
You've finished with machine-gun fire –
Knocked over in a hopeless dud-attack.

Somehow I always thought you'd get done in,
Because you were so desperate keen to live:
You were all out to try and save your skin,
Well knowing how much the world had got to give.
You joked at shells and talked the usual "shop,"
Stuck to your dirty job and did it fine:
With "Jesus Christ! When *will* it stop?
Three years . . . It's hell unless we break their line."

So when they told me you'd been left for dead
I wouldn't believe them, feeling it *must* be true.
Next week the bloody Roll of Honour said
"Wounded and missing" – (That's the thing to do
When lads are left in shell-holes dying slow,
With nothing but blank sky and wounds that ache,
Moaning for water till they know
It's night, and then it's not worth while to wake!)

Good-bye, old lad! Remember me to God,
And tell Him that our Politicians swear
They won't give in till Prussian Rule's been trod
Under the Heel of England . . . Are you there? . . .
Yes. . . and the War won't end for at least two years;
But we've got stacks of men . . . I'm blind with tears,
Staring into the dark. Cheero!
I wish they'd killed you in a decent show.

Mid-June, 1917

SIEGFRIED SASSOON DESERTS
WAR HERO TURNED PROTESTER

Siegfried Sassoon won the Military Cross for bombing and capturing a
German trench single-handed in June 1916. In August he was invalided
to England with trench fever.

He returned to France in February 1917. In April he was wounded in the
shoulder and sent to hospital in England.

While convalescing he discussed his growing disillusionment with the war with Bertrand Russell who encouraged him to make a daringly defiant protest in an attempt to influence public opinion and the Government. Sassoon decided to refuse to fight and not only to send his refusal to his commanding officer, but also to publish it as widely as possible. He threw his Military Cross into the River Mersey.

He prepared a protest statement which eventually was read in Parliament, and appeared in *The Times* on 31st July, 1917.

WILFUL DEFIANCE
OF MILITARY AUTHORITY

Sassoon's Protest Statement read in Parliament 30th July, 1917

I am making this statement as an act of wilful defiance of military authority, because I believe that the War is being deliberately prolonged by those who have the power to end it. I am a soldier, convinced that I am acting on behalf of soldiers.

I believe that this war, upon which I entered as a war of defence and liberation, has now become a war of aggression and conquest. I believe that the purpose for which I and my fellow soldiers entered upon this War should have been so clearly stated as to have made it impossible for them to be changed without our knowledge, and that, had this been done, the objects which actuated us would now be attainable by negotiation.

I have seen and endured the suffering of the troops, and I can no longer be a party to prolong those sufferings for ends which I believe to be evil and unjust.

I am not protesting against the military conduct of the War, but against the political errors and insincerities for which the fighting men are being sacrificed.

On behalf of those who are suffering now I make this protest against the deception which is being practised on them.Also I believe that it may help to destroy the callous complacence with which the majority of those at home regard the continuance of agonies which they do not share, and which they have not sufficient imagination to realise.

Sassoon expected to be put on trial and possibly shot.

He was ordered to appear before a medical board at Chester. He failed to appear. The next time he was ordered to appear before the board he did appear. His friend, Robert Graves, argued that Sassoon had gone mad. He had "seen corpses in the street"; he wanted to shoot the Prime Minister, and Sir Douglas Haig; and he had an irresistible urge to go back to fight and get himself killed. – Whether or not the board was persuaded by these arguments it seemed to give them an idea for defusing the publicity Sassoon was beginning to receive. He was ordered to a mental hospital – Craiglockhart War Hospital in Edinburgh which specialised in treating victims of shell shock. His doctor there, W H R Rivers declared him physically and mentally fit, but agreed to try to persuade Sassoon of the errors of his beliefs.

Sassoon's views of the war

I wish I could believe that Ancient War History justifies the indefinite prolongation of this war. The Jingoes define it as "an enormous quarrel between incompatible spirits and destinies, in which one or other must succumb." But the men who write these manifestos do not truly know what useless suffering the war inflicts.

And the ancient wars on which they base their arguments did not involve such huge sacrifices as the next two or three years will demand of Europe, if this war is to be carried on to a knock-out result.Our peace-terms remain the same, "the destruction of Kaiserism and Prussianism." I don't know what aims this destruction represents.

I only know, and declare from the depths of my agony, that these empty words (so often on the lips of the Jingoes) mean the destruction of Youth. They mean the whole torment of waste and despair which people refuse to acknowledge or to face; from month to month they dupe themselves with hopes that "the war will end this year."

And the Army is dumb. The Army goes on with its bitter tasks. The ruling classes do all the talking. And their words convince no one but the crowds *who are their dupes*.

The soldiers who return home seem to be stunned by the things they have endured. They are willingly entrapped by the silent conspiracy against them. They have come back to life from the door of death, and the world is good to enjoy. They vaguely know that it is "bad form" to hurt people's feelings by telling the truth about the war. Poor heroes! If only they would speak out;and throw their medals in the faces of their masters; and ask their women why it thrills them to know that they, the dauntless warriors, have shed the blood of Germans. Do not the women gloat secretly over the wounds of their lovers? Is there anything inwardly noble in savage sex instincts?

The rulers of England have always relied on the ignorance and patient credulity of the crowd. If the crowd could see into those cynical hearts it would lynch its dictators. For it is to the inherent weakness of human nature, and not to its promiscuous nobility, that these great men make their incessant appeals.

The soldiers are fooled by the popular assumption that they are all heroes. They have a part to play, a mask to wear. They are allowed to assume a pride of superiority to the mere civilian. Are there no heroes among the civilians, men and women alike?

Of the elderly male population I can hardly trust myself to speak. Their frame of mind is, in the majority of cases, intolerable. They glory in senseless invective against the enemy. They glory in the mock-heroism of their young men. They glory in the mechanical phrases of the Northcliffe Press. They regard the progress of the war like a game of chess, cackling about "attrition," and "wastage of man-power," and "civilisation at stake." In every class of society there are old men like ghouls, insatiable in their desire for slaughter, impenetrable in their ignorance.

Soldiers conceal their hatred of the war. Civilians conceal their liking for it.

"How vastly the spiritual gain of those who are left behind out-weighs the agony and loss of those who fight and die . . . the everlasting glory and exaltation of war." (From a review in *The Times Literary Supplement*.)

This is the sort of thing I am in revolt against. But I belong to "a war-wearied and bewildered minority" which regards "victory" and "defeat" as rhetorical terms with little precise meaning.

Diary, 19 June, 1917

On 15th June Sassoon had sent copies of his protest to over a dozen friends acquaintances and famous people – including the novelist, Arnold Bennet, who was employed by the British Government to write propaganda supporting the war.

Arnold Bennett argues against Sassoon

I think you are very misguided and that your position cannot be argumentatively defended . . . The point is that you are not in a situation to judge the situation. For you are not going to tell me that you have studied it in all its main bearings and branches. In my opinion a citizen is not justified in acting in such a way as will, so far as he is concerned, fundamentally thwart the desires of the majority as expressed by the accepted channels, unless he has with reasonable fullness acquainted himself with the facts of the case. If you were acting from an objection to all war, your position would be comprehensible and justifiable. But you are acting from an opinion that this particular war has reached a particular stage and that civilians have reached a particular degree of inhumanity. The overwhelming majority of your fellow citizens are against you. You may say that your action affects only yourself. Not so. It affects the whole State. You did not bind yourself as an officer on the understanding that you should be free from obligation whenever you happened to conclude that the war ought to be over. You are arrogating to yourself a right to which you are not entitled . . . I rely on you not to resent this epistle. Your suspicion is correct. The Army will ultimately lay it down that you are "daft." You aren't of course, but that's how it will end. What is the matter with you is spiritual pride.

Yours ever, A B
Letter to Siegfried Sassoon, 20 July, 1917.

FIGHT TO A FINISH

The boys came back. Bands played and flags were flying,
And Yellow-Pressmen[1] thronged the sunlit street
To cheer the soldiers who'd refrained from dying,
And hear the music of returning feet.
"Of all the thrills and ardours War has brought,
This moment is the finest." (So they thought.)

Snapping their bayonets on to charge the mob,
Grim Fusiliers[2] broke ranks with glint of steel,
At last the boys had found a cushy[3] job.

I heard the Yellow-Pressmen grunt and squeal;
And with my trusty bombers turned and went
To clear those Junkers[4] out of Parliament.

At Craiglockhart, July - November, 1917

1 cowardly journalists   2 soldiers   3 easy, soft   4 landed gentry who were keen supporters of a war (to defend their interests)

DOES IT MATTER?

Does it matter? – losing your legs?...
For people will always be kind,
And you need not show that you mind
When the others come in after hunting
To gobble their muffins and eggs.

Does it matter? – losing your sight? ...
There's such splendid work for the blind;
And people will always be kind,
As you sit on the terrace remembering
And turning your face to the light.

Do they matter? –   those dreams from the pit[1]? . .
You can drink and forget and be glad,
And people won't say that you're mad;
For they'll know that you've fought for your country
And no one will worry a bit.

At Craiglockhart, July - November, 1917

1 depths of misery and despair

GLORY OF WOMEN

You love us when we're heroes, home on leave,
Or wounded in a mentionable place.
You worship decorations; you believe
That chivalry redeems[1] the war's disgrace.
You make us shells. You listen with delight,
By tales of dirt and danger fondly thrilled.
You crown our distant ardours while we fight,
And mourn our laurelled[2] memories when we're killed.
You can't believe that British troops "retire"
When hell's last horror breaks them, and they run,
Trampling the terrible corpses - blind with blood.

O German mother dreaming by the fire,
While you are knitting socks to send your son
His face is trodden deeper in the mud.

At Craiglockhart, July - November, 1917

1 makes up for   2 crowned with a laurel wreath, the symbol of victory

PRELUDE:[1] THE TROOPS

Dim, gradual thinning of the shapeless gloom
Shudders to drizzling daybreak that reveals
Disconsolate men who stamp their sodden boots
And turn dulled, sunken faces to the sky
Haggard and hopeless. They, who have beaten down
The stale despair of night, must now renew
Their desolation in the truce of dawn,
Murdering the livid hours that grope for peace.

Yet these who cling to life with stubborn hands,
Can grin through storms of death and find a gap
In the clawed, cruel tangles of his defence.
They march from safety, and the bird-sung joy

Of grass-green thickets, to the land where all
Is ruin, and nothing blossoms but the sky
That hastens over them where they endure
Sad, smoking, flat horizons, reeking woods,
And foundered trench-lines volleying doom for doom.

O my brave brown companions, when your souls
Flock silently away, and the eyeless dead
Shame the wild beast of battle on the ridge,
Death will stand grieving in that field of war
Since your unvanquished[2] hardihood[3] is spent.
And through some mooned Valhalla[4] there will pass
Battalions and battalions, scarred from hell;
The unreturning army that was youth;
The legions who have suffered and are dust.

At Craiglockhart, July-November, 1917

1 introduction   2 unconquered   3 endurance, strength   4 mythical hall where soldier heroes who
died in battle live for evermore

ATTACK

At dawn the ridge emerges massed and dun[1]
In wild purple of the glow'ring[2] sun,
Smouldering through spouts of drifting smoke that shroud[3]
The menacing scarred slope; and, one by one,
Tanks creep and topple forward to the wire.
The barrage[4] roars and lifts. Then, clumsily bowed
With bombs and guns and shovels and battle-gear,
Men jostle and climb to meet the bristling fire.[5]
Lines of grey, muttering faces, masked with fear,
They leave their trenches, going over the top,
While time ticks blank and busy[6] on their wrists,
And hope,[7] with furtive[8] eyes and grappling[9] fists,
Flounders[10] in mud. O Jesus, make it stop!

At Craiglockhart, July-November, 1917

1 *massed and dun* - as a great mass 2 staring in anger 3 cover, like the death robes that cover a
corpse 4 continual firing of the big guns 5 *bristling fire* - the sharp points of fire from the guns
which are directed towards the men (like a lot of bristles) 6 *time ticks blank and busy* - perhaps
time passes quickly, but unnoticed by the men 7 the men who have hope, and hope itself
8 anxious, doubtful 9 trying to grab a firm hold on something 10 struggles with great difficulty

COUNTER-ATTACK[1]

We'd gained our first objective[2] hours before
While dawn broke like a face with blinking eyes,
Pallid, unshaved and thirsty, blind with smoke.
Things seemed all right at first. We held their line,
With bombers posted,[3] Lewis guns[4] well placed,
And clink of shovels deepening the shallow trench.
　　　The place was rotten with dead; green clumsy legs
　　　High-booted, sprawled and grovelled along the saps[5]
　　　And trunks, face downward, in the sucking mud,
　　　Wallowed like trodden sand-bags loosely filled;
　　　And naked sodden buttocks, mats of hair,
　　　Bulged, clotted heads slept in the plastering slime.
　　　And then the rain began, − the jolly old rain![6]

A yawning soldier knelt against the bank,
Staring across the morning blear with fog;
He wondered when the Allemands[7] would get busy;
And then, of course, they started with five-nines[8]
Traversing, sure as fate, and never a dud.[9]
Mute in the clamour of shells he watched them burst
Spouting dark earth and wire with gusts from hell,
While posturing[10] giants dissolved in drifts of smoke.
He crouched and flinched, dizzy with galloping fear,
Sick for escape, −   loathing the strangled horror
And butchered, frantic gestures of the dead.

An officer came blundering down the trench:
"Stand-to and man the fire step!" On he went . . .
Gasping and bawling, "Fire-step . . . counter-attack!"
Then the haze lifted. Bombing on the right
Down the old sap: machine guns on the left;
And stumbling figures looming out in front.
"O Christ, they're coming at us!" Bullets spat,
And he remembered his rifle . . . rapid fire . . .
And started blazing wildly . . . then a bang
Crumpled and spun him sideways, knocked him out
To grunt and wriggle: none heeded him; he choked
And fought the flapping veils of smothering gloom,
Lost in a blurred confusion of yells and groans . . .
Down, and down, and down, he sank and drowned,
Bleeding to death. The counter-attack had failed.

At Craiglockhart, July-November, 1917, from a July 1916 draft.

---

1 *COUNTER-ATTACK* - an attack made in reply to an earlier attack. In this case, the Germans were
trying to recapture their own trenches just lost to the British   2 *gained our first objective* - captured
the part of the enemy trench that we had set out to capture   3 positioned   4 *Lewis guns* - British

machine-guns   5 trenches running forward from the front line, towards the enemy   6 exceptional
rainfall during the First World War, turned battlefields into incredible sticky swamps of mud
7 Germans   8 *five-nines* - large explosive shells   9 failure (in this case a shell that doesn't
explode)   10 posing

SASSOON CHANGES HIS MIND

A number of Sassoon's friends had written to him criticising his behav-
iour, and Rivers pointed out to him how safe Sassoon was compared with
the men under his command. After four months Sassoon's sense of guilt
about not fighting alongside other soldiers became too much for him.
He wrote:

> At the front I should find forgetfulness. And I would rather be
> killed than survive as one who wangled his way through by saying
> that the War ought to stop.

He asked to be sent back to the front line. By this time he and Rivers
had become friends and Rivers helped him to be passed as fit for battle
duty – even though he refused to change his criticisms of the way the
war was being "needlessly prolonged." On 26th November 1917 he left
the hospital to return to the battlefront. After a spell in camp in Ireland
he was sent to fight in Palestine on 8th February 1918.

BANISHMENT[1]

I am banished from the patient men who fight.
They smote my heart to pity, built my pride.
Shoulder to aching shoulder, side by side,
They trudged away from life's broad wealds[2] of light.
Their wrongs were mine; and ever in my sight
They went arrayed in honour. But they died –
Not one by one; and mutinous I cried
To those who sent them out into the night.

The darkness tells how vainly I have striven
To free them from the pit[3] where they must dwell
In outcast gloom convulsed[4] and jagged[5] and riven[6]
By grappling[7] guns. Love drove me to rebel.
Love drives me back to grope with them through hell;
And in their tortured eyes I stand forgiven.

At Craiglockhart, July-November, 1917

1 exile, being sent away   2 open countryside   3 battlefields   4 shaken by explosions   5 probably
referring to the war-torn landscape   6 torn apart, destroyed   7 struggling (usually refers to men
struggling in close combat)

Suicide

Hundreds of young men could not face the horror of war and killed themselves. How many did this will never be known as it was common practice to record such deaths as "killed in action."

Usual sort of letter

On his first night in the front line, Robert Graves came across a man, face down in the mud who refused to respond to orders. When Graves had a closer look with his torch he saw that the man had used his rifle to shoot himself through the head by putting the muzzle in his mouth and pushing the trigger with his toe.

Two Irish officers who came up told him that they had had several suicides recently and gave orders that the next of kin should be informed. "Usual sort of letter; tell them he died a soldier's death, anything you like. I'm not going to report it as suicide."

SUICIDE IN THE TRENCHES

I knew a simple soldier boy
Who grinned at life in empty joy,
Slept soundly through the lonesome dark,
And whistled early with the lark.

In winter trenches, cowed and glum,
With crumps[1] and lice and lack of rum,[2]
He put a bullet through his brain.
No-one spoke of him again.

You smug-faced crowds with kindling[3] eye
Who cheer when soldier lads march by,[4]
Sneak home and pray you'll never know
The hell where youth and laughter go.

Published 23 February, 1918

1 the noise made by shells falling in soft earth   2 *lack of rum* - rum was given to the troops,
sometimes before an attack and sometimes after, to steady nerves, increase confidence and numb
feelings.   3 shining, enthusiastic   4 *when soldier lads march by* - this probably refers to the
enthusiastic parades of new soldiers marching through town and city centres before going off to fight

REMORSE

Lost in the swamp and welter of the pit,[1]
He flounders off the duck-boards; only he knows
Each flash and spouting crash[2] – each instant lit
When gloom reveals the streaming rain. He goes
Heavily, blindly on. And, while he blunders,
"Could anything be worse than this?" – he wonders,
Remembering how he saw those Germans run,
Screaming for mercy among the stumps of trees:
Green-faced, they dodged and darted: there was one
Livid with terror, clutching at his knees . . .
Our chaps were sticking 'em like pigs . . . "Oh Hell!"
He thought – "there's things in war one dare not tell
Poor father sitting safe at home, who reads
Of dying heroes and their deathless deeds[3]."

At Limerick, Ireland, 4 February, 1918

1 the trench or battle   2 *spouting crash* - the exploding shell landing, sent up a fountain of water
and mud   3 *deathless deeds* - actions, the fame of which will live forever

RETURN TO FRANCE

On 9th May 1918 Sassoon's battalion arrived to fight in France.

I STOOD WITH THE DEAD

I stood with the Dead, so forsaken and still:
When dawn was grey I stood with the Dead.
And my slow heart said, "You must kill; you must kill:
Soldier, soldier, morning is red."

On the shapes of the slain in their crumpled disgrace
I stared for a while through the thin cold rain . . .
"O lad that I loved, there is rain on your face,
And your eyes are blurred[1] and sick like the plain."

I stood with the Dead . . . They were dead; they were dead;
My heart and my head beat a march of dismay;
And gusts of the wind came dulled[2] by the guns.
"Fall in[3]!" I shouted; "Fall in for your pay!"

Habarcq, 18 June, 1918

1 *blurred* - perhaps blurred with the rain water that had collected in them, or possibly the poet has
tears in his eyes; therefore the soldier's eyes look as misty as the rain-swept plain   2 the guns
sounded dull or muffled because they were a long way off

On 27th June Sassoon's volume of poetry, *Counter-Attack*, was pub-
lished. A few days later, on 13th July 1918, he was shot in the head,
by accident, by one of his own men. The bullet grazed, rather than
entered, his head.

He was sent home again to England on sick leave for the remaining
months of the war.

GREAT MEN

The great ones of the earth
Approve, with smiles and bland salutes, the rage
And monstrous tyranny they have brought to birth.
The great ones of the earth
Are much concerned about the wars they wage,
And quite aware of what those wars are worth.

You Marshals, gilt and red,
You Ministers and Princes, and Great Men,
Why can't you keep your mouthings for the dead?
Go round the simple cemeteries; and then
Talk of our noble sacrifice and losses
To the wooden crosses.

Published 17 August, 1918

AFTER THE WAR

RECONCILIATION

When you are standing at your hero's grave,
Or near some homeless village where he died,
Remember, through your heart's rekindling pride,
The German soldiers who were loyal and brave.

Men fought like brutes; and hideous things were done;
And you have nourished hatred harsh and blind.
But in that Golgotha[1] perhaps you'll find
The mothers of the men who killed your son.

November, 1918

1 literally, place where Christ was crucified; burial ground

MEMORIAL TABLET (Great War)

Squire nagged and bullied till I went to fight,
(Under Lord Derby's Scheme[1]). I died in hell —
(They called it Passchendaele). My wound was slight,
And I was hobbling back; and then a shell
Burst slick upon the duck-boards: so I fell
Into the bottomless mud, and lost the light.

At sermon-time, while Squire is in his pew,
He gives my gilded name a thoughtful stare;
For, though low down upon the list, I'm there;
"*In proud and glorious memory*" . . . that's my due.
Two bleeding years I fought in France, for Squire:
I suffered anguish that he's never guessed.
Once I came home on leave: and then went west[2] . . .
What greater glory could a man desire?

    November, 1918

1 *Lord Derby's Scheme* - Lord Derby's Scheme invited men to volunteer for the army promising
them that they would be able to stay with their friends who volunteered. These men went into the
"pals" batallions   2 *went west* - slang expression meaning died, or, was killed

VICARIOUS CHRIST

The Bishop of Byegumb[1] was an old friend of our General;
In fact he knew him out in the Soudan.[2]
He preached to our Brigade; and the impression that he made
Was astounding; he was such a Christian man.

He compared us to the martyrs who were burnt alive and strangled;
O, it made us love the war – to hear him speak!
"The Americans[3]," he said, "are coming over in large numbers;
And the Huns are getting weaker every week."

The Bishop of Byegumb has preached on Victory, I am certain,
(Though I haven't seen it mentioned in the Press).
But when I was his victim, how I wished I could have kicked him,
For he made me love Religion less and less.

Published 1 February, 1919

1 by gum! is a very mild form of swearing. Sassoon's use of something like it for a name is no
doubt intended to suggest something about the character of the bishop   2 Sudan, a country in
north-east Africa. The British fought there at the end of the 19th century.   3 American troops
under General Pershing began to arrive in France on the 26th of June, 1917. Up to a million were
expected in total.

An example of views on warfare expressed by a leading member of the Christian church in Britain

War is not murder. . . war is sacrifice. The fighting and killing
are not of the essence of it, but are the accidents, though the
inseparable accidents; and even those in the wide modern fields
where a soldier rarely in his own sight sheds any blood but his
own, where he lies on the battle sward not to inflict death but to
endure it - even these are mainly purged of savagery and

transfigured into devotion. War is not murder but sacrifice,
which is the soul of Christianity.

> Canon J.H Skrine of Merton College, Oxford,
> in a National Service League pamphlet.

EVERYONE SANG

Everyone suddenly burst out singing;
And I was filled with such delight
As prisoned birds must find in freedom,
Winging wildly across the white
Orchards and dark-green fields; on - on - and out
Of sight.

Everyone's voice was suddenly lifted;
And beauty came like the setting sun:
My heart was shaken with tears; and horror
Drifted away. . . O, but Everyone
Was a bird; and the song was wordless; the singing will
Never be done.

April, 1919

ON PASSING THE NEW MENIN GATE

Who will remember, passing through this Gate,
The unheroic Dead who fed the guns?
Who shall absolve[1] the foulness of their fate, –
Those doomed, conscripted, unvictorious ones?

Crudely renewed, the Salient[2] holds its own.
Paid are its dim defenders by this pomp;
Paid, with a pile of peace-complacent stone,
The armies who endured that sullen swamp.

Here was the world's worst wound. And here with pride
"Their name liveth for ever," the Gateway claims.
Was ever an immolation[3] so belied[4]
As these intolerably nameless names?
Well might the Dead who struggled in the slime
Rise and deride this sepulchre of crime.

Begun Brussels, 25 July 1927; finished London, January, 1928.

---

1 wash away   2 the Ypres Salient where the Menin Gate is situated; the miles of battlefields to the
east of Ypres which include Langemark, Passchendael and Messines   3 sacrifice   4 misrepresented

The Menin Gate Memorial, Ypres, Belgium.

Sassoon predicted that the soldiers would be forgotten, but the war, the dead, the suffering, the loss have not been forgotten. Inscribed on the stonework of the gate are the names of 54,896 soldiers, "officers and men who died in the Ypres Salient but to whom the fortunes of war denied the honoured and known burial given to their comrades in death." Every evening at 8pm before a gathering that may be just a small handful, or, on special occasions can be as large as 3000, trumpeters sound the last post. They have done this since July 1927, when the memorial was inaugurated, and will do for all time. – However, the dead may still have cause to deride this monument because wars have continued on a massive and horrific scale since the First World War, mainly with weapons developed and supplied by the so-called civilised nations who were believed to have learned lessons from the tragic mistakes of 1914-1918.

COMMENTS ON THE POETRY OF SASSOON

Sassoon on his poetry

Many of my shorter poems have been written with a sense of emotional release and then perfected by revision – often after being put away for a long time. Others have been produced by mental concentration and word seeking which lasted two or three hours. But there was usually a feeling of having said what I wanted to with directness and finality.

Why can't they realize that the war poems were improvised by an impulsive, intolerant, immature young creature, under extreme stress of experience?

I should say myself that the essential quality (of my poems) is that I have been true to what I experienced. All the best ones are truly experienced and therefore authentic in expression.

Wilfred Owen on Sassoon

Nothing like his trench life sketches has ever been written or ever will be written. Shakespeare reads vapid after these.

H.W Massingham on Sassoon

These war-verses are not poetry . . . they are epigrams – modern epigrams, thrown deliberately into the harsh, peremptory, colloquial kind of versification which we have so often mistaken for poetry.

Virginia Woolf on Sassoon

We know no other writer who has shown us as effectually as Mr Sassoon the terrible pictures which lie behind the colourless phrases of the newspapers. Mr Sassoon's poems are too much in the key of the gramaphone at present, too fiercely suspicious of any comfort or compromise, to be read as poetry; but his contempt for palliative or subterfuge gives us the raw stuff of poetry.

Bernard Bergonzi on Sassoon

Sassoon remains fundamentally a poet of narrow but direct effects: his language is hard, clear, sharply defined, rather than suggestive or capable of the associative effects of a poet of larger resources. On the whole, Sassoon did not attempt a profundity that was beyond him; his gifts were, pre-eminently, those of a satirist, and it was in satire that he excelled.

Nevertheless these poems, expressing a mood of anti-heroic revolt with such fervour and harsh wit, strike a new and incisive note in the literature of war. . . sometimes these poems rise to an unusual level of poetic intensity, as in *On Passing the New Menin Gate*.

Dominic Hibberd and John Onions on Sassoon

Sassoon is unique. He is a key figure . . . since his writing records his changing views with a sincerity and continuity that no other poet's work can match.

12

ISAAC ROSENBERG 1890 - 1918

EARLY ATTITUDES TO THE WAR

Because of a chest complaint Rosenberg was on holiday in Africa in August 1914. When war was declared he wrote to his friend Edward Marsh, "By the time you get this the war will only just have begun, I'm afraid. Europe will have stepped into its bath of blood."

Although he was unsuited to military service – being very small, very absent-minded and having weak lungs – he volunteered to fight at the end of October, 1915, two months before conscription was brought in. He had failed to get sufficient work as an artist, and had been encouraged by the news that half of his pay as a soldier could be sent to his mother.

His attempt to join the Royal Army Medical Corps as a stretcher bearer, was rejected because he was so tiny. He served as a private in the Bantam Battalion of 12th Suffolk Regiment where he complained of "bulleyisms" and punishments for forgetting things (such as carrying his gas mask). He described army life as ridiculous, idiotic and mean-ingless – controlled by puny minds. – In late December he wrote to Edward Marsh,

> I never joined the army from patriotic reasons. Nothing can justify war. I suppose we must all fight to get the trouble over.

ON RECEIVING NEWS OF WAR

Snow is a strange white word.
No ice or frost
Has asked of bud or bird
For Winter's cost.

Yet ice and frost and snow
From earth to sky
This Summer land doth know.
No man knows why.

In all men's hearts it is.
Some spirit old
Hath turned with malign kiss
Our lives to mould.

Red fangs have torn His face.
God's blood is shed.
He mourns from His lone place
His children dead.

O! ancient crimson curse!
Corrode,[1] consume.
Give back this universe
Its pristine[2] bloom.

Capetown, 1914

1 eat away, bit by bit, like an acid dissolving, for example, a metal   2 original, perfect

AUGUST 1914

What in our lives is burnt
In the fire of this?
The heart's dear granary?[1]
The much we shall miss?

Three lives hath one life—
Iron, honey, gold.
The gold, the honey gone—
Left is the hard and cold.

Iron are our lives
Molten right through our youth.
A burnt space through ripe fields,
A fair mouth's broken tooth.

1916

1 the place where grain (food and seed for the future) is stored

FRONT LINE POEMS

BREAK OF DAY IN THE TRENCHES

The darkness crumbles away.
It is the same old druid Time as ever,
Only a live thing leaps my hand,
A queer sardonic rat,
As I pull the parapet's poppy
To stick behind my ear.
Droll rat, they would shoot you if they knew
Your cosmopolitan sympathies.
Now you have touched this English hand
You will do the same to a German
Soon, no doubt, if it be your pleasure
To cross the sleeping green between.
It seems you inwardly grin as you pass
Strong eyes, fine limbs, haughty athletes,
Less chanced[1] than you for life,
Bonds to the whims of murder,
Sprawled in the bowels of the earth,
The torn fields of France.
What do you see in our eyes
At the shrieking iron and flame
Hurled through still heavens?
What quaver — what heart aghast?
Poppies whose roots are in man's veins
Drop, and are ever dropping;
But mine in my ear is safe —
Just a little white with the dust.

June, 1916

1 *Less chanced* - less likely to have a chance of life

IN THE TRENCHES

I snatched two poppies
From the parapet's ledge,
Two bright red poppies
That winked on the ledge.
Behind my ear
I stuck one through,
One blood red poppy
I gave to you.

The sandbags narrowed
And screwed out our jest,
And tore the poppy
You had on your breast . . .
Down – a shell – O! Christ,
I am choked . . .safe . . . dust blind, I
See trench floor poppies
Strewn. Smashed you lie.

1916

THE DYING SOLDIER

"Here are houses," he moaned,
"I could reach, but my brain swims."[1]
Then they thundered and flashed
And shook the earth to its rims.

"They are gunpits,"[2] he gasped,
"Our men are at the guns.
Water! –Water! – Oh, water!
For one of England's dying sons."

"We cannot give you water,
Were all England in your breath."
"Water! – Water! – Oh water!"
He moaned and swooned[3] to death.

1916?

1 is dizzy   2 shallow excavations for the big field guns   3 lost consciousness, fainted

DEAD MAN'S DUMP

The plunging limbers[1] over the shattered track
Racketed[2] with their rusty freight,
Stuck out like many crowns of thorns,
And the rusty stakes like sceptres old
To stay the flood of brutish men
Upon our brothers dear.

The wheels lurched over sprawled dead
But pained them not, though their bones crunched.
Their shut mouths made no moan.
They lie there huddled, friend and foeman,
Man born of man, and born of woman,
And shells go crying over them
From night till night and now.

Earth has waited for them
All the time of their growth
Fretting for their decay:
Now she has them at last!
In the strength of their strength
Suspended — stopped and held.

What fierce imaginings their dark souls lit!
Earth! have they gone into you?
Somewhere they must have gone,
And flung on your hard back
Is their souls' sack,
Emptied of God-ancestralled essences.[3]
Who hurled them out? Who hurled?

None saw their spirits' shadow shake the grass,
Or stood aside for the half used life to pass
Out of those doomed nostrils and the doomed mouth,
When the swift iron burning bee
Drained the wild honey[4] of their youth.

What of us, who flung on the shrieking pyre,
Walk, our usual thoughts untouched,
Our lucky limbs as on ichor[5] fed,
Immortal seeming ever?
Perhaps when the flames beat loud on us,
A fear may choke in our veins
And the startled blood may stop.

The air is loud with death;
The dark air spurts with fire;
The explosions ceaseless are.
Timelessly now, some minutes past,
These dead strode time with vigorous life,
Till the shrapnel called "an end!"
But not to all. In bleeding pangs
Some borne on stretchers dreamed of home,
Dear things, war-blotted from their hearts.

A man's brains splattered on
A stretcher-bearer's face;
His shook shoulders slipped their load,
But when they bent to look again
The drowning soul was sunk too deep
For human tenderness.

They left this dead with the older dead,
Stretched at the cross roads.

Burnt black by strange decay,
Their sinister faces lie
The lid over each eye.
The grass and coloured clay
More motion have than they,
Joined to the great sunk silences.

Here is one not long dead;
His dark hearing caught our far wheels,
And the choked soul stretched weak hands
To reach the living word, the far wheels said.[6]
The blood-dazed intelligence beating for light,
Crying through the suspense of the far torturing wheels
Swift for the end to break,
Or the wheels to break,
Cried as the tide of the world broke over his sight.

Will they come? Will they ever come?
Even as the mixed hoofs of the mules,
The quivering-bellied mules,
And the rushing wheels all mixed
With his tortured upturned sight,
So we crashed round the bend,
We heard his weak scream,
We heard his very last sound,
And our wheels grazed his dead face.

May, 1917

1 wagons   2 making a dreadful noise   3 *God-ancestralled essences* - essential qualities inherited
from God   4 *wild honey* - zest for life, youthful spirit   5 *limbs as on ichor fed* - limbs having a
supernatural power to live; veins flowing with the blood of the gods (of Ancient Greek mythology)
6 Rosenberg's punctuation of this line lacked a comma after *word*, and had a comma after *said.*

MANIAC EARTH!

Maniac Earth! howling and flying your bowel
Seared by the jagged fire, the iron love
The impetuous storm of savage love.
Dark Earth! dark heaven, swinging in chemic smoke
What dead are born when you kiss each soundless soul
With lightning and thunder from your mined[1] heart,
Which man's self dug, and his blind fingers loosed.

May, 1917

1 containing one explosive mine

Maniac Earth! was originally the ninth stanza of Rosenberg's *Dead Man's Dump*. It was omitted from his final version of that poem, presumably because it broke up the flow of ideas.

THE IMMORTALS

I killed them, but they would not die.
Yea! All the day and all the night
For them I could not rest nor sleep,
Nor guard from them nor hide in flight.

Then in my agony I turned
And made my hands red in their gore.
In vain — for faster than I slew
They rose more cruel than before.

I killed and killed with slaughter mad;
I killed till all my strength was gone.
And still they rose to torture me,
For Devils only die in fun.

I used to think the Devil hid
In women's smiles and wine's carouse.[1]
I called him Satan, Balzebub.[2]
But now I call him, dirty louse.

1917

1 *wine's carouse* - drinking too much wine   2 *Satan, Balzebub* - names of the Devil

RETURNING, WE HEAR THE LARKS

Sombre the night is.
And though we have our lives, we know
What sinister threat lurks there.

Dragging these anguished limbs, we only know
This poison-blasted track opens on our camp —
On a little safe sleep.

But hark! joy — joy — strange joy.
Lo! heights of night ringing with unseen larks.
Music showering our upturned list'ning faces.

Death could drop from the dark
As easily as song —
But song only dropped,

Like a blind man's dreams on the sand
By dangerous tides,
Like a girl's dark hair for she dreams no ruin lies there,
Or her kisses where a serpent hides.

1917

LOUSE HUNTING

Nudes - stark and glistening,
Yelling in lurid glee. Grinning faces
And raging limbs
Whirl over the floor one fire.
For a shirt verminously busy
Yon soldier tore from his throat, with oaths
Godhead might shrink at, but not the lice.
And soon the shirt was aflare
Over the candle he'd lit while we lay.

Then we all sprang up and stript
To hunt the verminous brood.
Soon like a demon's pantomime
The place was raging.
See the silhouettes agape,
See the gibbering shadows
Mixed with the battled arms on the wall.
See gargantuan hooked fingers
Pluck in supreme flesh[1]
To smutch supreme littleness.[2]
See the merry limbs in hot Highland fling[3]
Because some wizard vermin
Charmed from the quiet this revel[4]
When our ears were half lulled
By the dark music
Blown from Sleep's trumpet.

1917

---

1 *supreme flesh* - flesh of the highest ranking being (man)   2 *supreme littleness* - extreme
littleness   3 dance   4 wild celebration

COMMENTS ON THE POETRY OF ISAAC ROSENBERG

Isaac Rosenberg on poetry

I think that poetry should be definite thought and clear
expression, however subtle; I don't think there should be any

vagueness at all; but a sense of something hidden and felt to be there.

Siegfried Sassoon on Rosenberg's poems

I have been strongly impressed by their depth and integrity. I have found a sensitive and vigorous mind energetically interested in experimenting with language. . . His experiments were a strenuous effort for impassioned expression; his imagination had a sinewy and muscular aliveness; often he saw things in terms of sculpture. . . I find him a poet of movement; words which express movement are often used by him and are essential to his natural utterance. . . words and images obey him, instead of leading into over-elaboration.

Bernard Bergonzi on Rosenberg

Isaac Rosenberg was one of the finest of the war poets. . . (He) was distinguished from the other war poets by his Jewish origins and his urban working-class background, which meant he had no English pastoral nostalgia to set against front-line experience.

Jon Silkin on Rosenberg

Rosenberg's strength as a 'war poet' arises partly from his ability to particularise powerful physical horror and take it, without losing its presence, to a further stage of consciousness.

13

WILFRED OWEN 1893 –1918

At the outbreak of the war Wilfred Owen was twenty-one. He was living in France, at Bagnères-de-Bigorre, six miles from the foot of the Pyrenees and twelve from Lourdes, earning his living as a private tutor, teaching English to French children. His distance from the action may have helped him to feel little concern about the fighting in and near Belgium. For many months he rarely mentioned the war in his numerous personal letters.

MY LIFE IS WORTH MORE THAN MY DEATH TO ENGLISHMEN.

When he first mentioned the war in letters it was near the end of August.

> The war affects me less than it ought . . . I can do no service to anybody by agitating for news or making dole over the slaughter... I feel my own life all the more precious and more dear in the presence of this deflowering of Europe.

However, he was not immune to its effects, for in September he visited a local hospital with his friend, Doctor Sauvaître, to see the French and German war wounded who were being brought in. To "educate" his brother, Harold, "to the actualities of war" he described in detail some of the wounds and operations he saw — completing the letter with little sketches of injuries.

Nevertheless, he did write one pro-war poem at that time: *The Ballad of Purchase Money* which contains this verse:

> O meet[1] it is and passing[2] sweet[3]
> To live in peace with others,
> But sweeter still and far more meet
> To die in war for brothers.

1 right   2 extremely   3 pleasing

On 2nd December 1914 he wrote to his mother,

> The *Daily Mail* speaks very movingly about the "duties shirked"
> by English young men. I suffer a good deal of shame. But while
> those ten thousand lusty louts go on playing football I shall go on
> playing with my little axiom:- that my life is worth more than my
> death to Englishmen.

1914

> War broke: and now the Winter of the world
> With perishing great darkness closes in.
> The foul tornado, centred at Berlin,
> Is over all the width of Europe whirled,
> Rending the sails of progress. Rent or furled
> Are all Art's ensigns.[1] Verse wails. Now begin
> Famines of thought and feeling. Love's wine's thin.
> The grain[2] of human Autumn rots, down-hurled.
>
> For after Spring had bloomed in early Greece,[3]
> And Summer blazed her glory out with Rome,[4]
> An Autumn softly fell, a harvest home,
> A slow grand age, and rich with all increase.
> But now, for us, wild Winter, and the need
> Of sowings for new Spring, and blood for seed.

> Drafted in southern France in late 1914.

1 literally flags; here *Art's ensigns* symbolise artistic works and activities   2 literally seed corn ;
various interpretations are possible along the line of 'man's hope for the future.'   3 *Spring had
bloomed in early Greece* - Greek civilization, one of the earliest, is seen as the Springtime of
mankind   4 *And Summer blazed her glory out with Rome* - Roman civilization is seen as the
Summertime of mankind

ENLISTMENT

Eventually, on 15th May 1915, Owen returned to England and encoun-
tered all the psychological pressures to enlist. His brother Harold, wrote
of this experience:

> being branded with lack of courage and the ostracism which
> would follow − this prospect and all its consequences he found
> appalling, and much more frightening than the horrid thought of
> army discipline.

He returned to France on 11th June, and came back to England on 14th
September to enlist. This he finally did on 21st October.

He revealed in a letter to his mother, dated 2nd November 1915, his chief pleasure in being a soldier:

> Walking abroad, one is the admiration of all little boys, and meets an approving glance from every eye of eld.

Wilfred Owen's preparation for front line duties

On the 15th November 1915 Wilfred Owen went into training as Cadet Owen, Artists' Rifles at Hare Hall Camp, Gidea Park, Essex. He continued his training in England throughout 1916. On the 4th of June, 1916 he was commissioned into the Manchester Regiment. On the 18th he joined the fifth (Reserve) Battalion, Manchester Regiment, at Milford Camp, near Witley, Surrey before doing further training in Aldershot, Farnborough, Oswestry (under canvas), Southport, Lancashire and Fleetwood.

The following poem was probably written as a reply to Rupert Brooke's *The Soldier.*

AN IMPERIAL ELEGY

Not one corner of a foreign field
But a span as wide as Europe;
An appearance of a titan's grave,
And the length thereof a thousand miles,
It crossed all Europe like a mystic road,
Or as the Spirits' Pathway lieth on the night.
And I heard a voice crying
This is the Path of Glory.

September 1915-May?1916

This next poem, written while still training in England, may be one of the poems Sassoon described as having "an almost embarrassing sweetness of sentiment." Ideas for it were to re-emerge in *Exposure* and *Anthem for Doomed Youth.*

TO A COMRADE IN FLANDERS

Seeing we never spied frail Fairyland,
Though small we crouched by bluebells, moon by moon,
And are too late for Lethe's[1] tide; too soon
For that new bridge that leaves old Styx[2] half-spanned:
Nor meekly unto Mecca[3] caravanned;
Nor bugled Asgard,[4] skilled in magic rune;
Nor yearned for far Nirvana,[5] the sweet swoon;
And are from Paradise[6] cursed out and banned:

Let's die back to those hearths we died for. Thus
Shall we be gods there. Death shall be no sev'rance.
In dull, dim chancels, flower new shrines for us.
For us, rough knees of boys shall ache with rev'rance;
For girls' breasts are the clear white Acropole[7]
Where our own mothers' tears shall heal us whole.

September, 1916

1 a river in the "underworld" in Greek mythology. To drink its water caused forgetfullness
2 a river in the "underworld" in Greek mythology across which the souls of the dead were ferried
3 the holiest city of Islam   4 a dwelling place of Gods in Norse mythology   5 in Buddhism the
blessed state of the ending of all desires   6 heaven   7 Acropolis? hilltop in Athens on which an
ancient Greek temple stands.

THE END

After the blast of lightning from the east,
The flourish of loud clouds, the Chariot Throne;
After the drums of time have rolled and ceased,
And by the bronze west long retreat is blown,
Shall life renew these bodies? Of a truth,
All death will he annul, all tears assuage?
Or fill these void veins full again with youth,
And wash, with an immortal water, age?

When I do ask white Age, he saith not so:
"My head hangs weighed with snow."
And when I hearken to the Earth, she saith:
"My fiery heart shrinks, aching. It is death.
Mine ancient scars shall not be glorified,
Nor my titanic[1] tears, the seas, be dried."

Late 1916, with revisions October 1917 - January, 1918.

1 the titans were the gigantic children of the gods, Uranus and Gaea, in Greek mythology; gigantic

On the 30th of December 1916 Wilfred Owen sailed for France.

THE SHOCK OF WAR

No knowledge, imagination or training fully prepared Owen for the
shock and suffering of front line experience. Within twelve days of ar-
riving in France the easy-going chatter of his letters turned to a cry of
anguish. By the 9th of January, 1917 he had joined the 2nd Manchesters

on the Somme – at Bertrancourt near Amien. Here he took command of number 3 platoon, "A" Company.

> I can see no excuse for deceiving you about these last four days. I have suffered seventh hell. – I have not been at the front. – I have been in front of it. – I held an advanced post, that is, a "dug-out" in the middle of No Man's Land.
>
> We had a march of three miles over shelled road, then nearly three along a flooded trench. After that we came to where the trenches had been blown flat out and had to go over the top. It was of course dark, too dark, and the ground was not mud, not sloppy mud, but an octopus of sucking clay, three, four, and five feet deep, relieved only by craters full of water . . .
>
> Three quarters dead. . . we reached the dug-out, and relieved the wretches therein . . .
>
> My dug-out held twenty-five men tight packed. Water filled it to a depth of one or two feet, leaving say four feet of air. One entrance had been blown in and blocked. – So far, the other remained.
>
> The Germans knew we were staying there and decided we shouldn't. Those fifty hours were the agony of my happy life. – Every ten minutes on Sunday afternoon seemed an hour. – I nearly broke down and let myself drown in the water that was now slowly rising over my knees.
>
> Towards 6 o'clock, when, I suppose, you would be going to church, the shelling grew less intense and less accurate: so that I was mercifully helped to do my duty and crawl, wade, climb and flounder over No Man's Land to visit my other post. It took me half an hour to move about a hundred and fifty yards . . .
>
> In the platoon on my left the sentries over the dug-out were blown to nothing . . . I kept my own sentries half way down the stairs during the most terrific bombardment. In spite of this, one lad was blown down and, I am afraid, blinded.

Letter to his mother, Susan Owen, 16 January, 1917.

Some of the experiences mentioned in this letter were later to feature in *The Sentry* and *Dulce et Decorum Est*, but these and other of Owen's great poems were still to be written. At this time he had not even considered writing poetry based directly on his war experiences and he had not settled on a mode of writing that matched his subject matter.

The winter of early 1917

In France it was the coldest winter anyone could remember, with the landscape covered in deep snow and ponds frozen ten inches thick. In Paris a temperature of minus 14 degrees Celsius was registered. It was impossible to keep soldiers out in the open in front line trenches for more than forty-eight hours at a time before taking a turn in the warmth and comfort of billets. Without this, whole armies would have died of exposure. Even so, soldiers suffered severely from frostbite, bronchitis, pneumonia, and rheumatism.

Background to *The Show* and *Exposure*

On the 19th January 1917 Owen wrote to his mother expressing ideas which emerged in his poem *The Show*.

> No Man's Land . . . is pock-marked like a body of foulest disease and its odour is the breath of cancer.

> I have not seen any dead. I have done worse. In the dank air I have perceived it, and in the darkness felt. . . No Man's Land under the snow is like the face of the moon chaotic, crater-ridden, uninhabitable, awful, the abode of madness. . . The people of England needn't hope. They must agitate.

Owen's experience at this time form the background to his poem *Exposure*. He wrote to his mother on the 4th of February 1917, saying that his latest experience was "almost wusser" than the first because his platoon, lacking dugouts, had to lie in the snow "marooned in a frozen desert." They suffered from thirst because their tiny army cookers were inadequate to melt the snow. One of his men died of exposure and others had to be taken to hospital.

OWEN DEVELOPS SHELL-SHOCK

On the 14th of March, 1917, Owen was finding his way in complete darkness when he fell through a shell hole in a floor and hit his head falling into a deep cellar. He suffered from concussion – headache, fever, vomiting and muscular pains. He was moved into a makeshift hospital quite near the front line where he rested, in good spirits, until returning to his company.

On 4th April he went back into action near St Quentin, and for four days and four nights he was out in the open in snow under heavy shelling, and had no sleep at all. A four day break was followed by return to action at Savy Wood. It was between here and the village of Fayet that Owen and his battalion marched over a hill top and through a hurricane barrage. Owen himself, to his amazement, was completely untouched by the storm of steel.

For twelve days they were in action or lay in holes under fire unable to sleep. One night, when Owen and his men were resting on a railway embankment a shell landed two yards from his head. He was blown in the air and landed some distance from the embankment. For several days he lay under a corrugated iron sheet close to a dead officer.

On 1st May his commanding officer noticed that Owen's speech was confused and that he trembled uncontrollably. He sent Owen to number 13 Casualty Clearing Station with shell-shock.

Writing from the clearing station on the 14th of May to his brother, Colin, Owen described his experiences in one of the April attacks. His poem, *Spring Offensive* is based on this remarkable occasion.

Wilfred Owen on "going over the top"

> The sensations of going over the top are about as exhilarating as those dreams of falling over a precipice, when you see the rocks at the bottom surging up to you . . . There was an extraordinary exultation in the act of slowly walking forward, showing ourselves openly. There was no bugle and no drum for which I was very sorry . . . Then we were caught in a tornado of shells. The various "waves" were all broken up and we carried on like a crowd moving off a cricket field. When I looked back and saw the ground all crawling and wormy with wounded bodies, I felt no horror at all but only an immense exultation at having got through the barrage.

WILFRED OWEN'S CONSCIENCE

Christian Duty

> I am more and more Christian as I walk the unchristian ways of Christendom. Already I have comprehended a light which never will filter into the dogma of any national church: namely that one of Christ's essential commands was: Passivity at any price! Suffer dishonour and disgrace; but never resort to arms. Be bullied, be outraged, be killed; but do not kill. It may be chimerical and an ignominious principle, but there it is. It can only be ignored: and I think pulpit professionals are ignoring it very skilfully and successfully indeed. . .
>
> Am I not myself a conscientious objector with a very seared conscience?

Christ is literally in no man's land. There men often hear His voice: Greater love hath no man than this, that a man lay down his life — for a friend.

Is it spoken in English only, and French?

I do not believe so.

Thus you see how pure Christianity will not fit in with pure patriotism.

                    Wilfred Owen, in a letter c.16 May, 1917.

Shell shock victim returns to England

In June 1917, Owen was taken first to Etretat and then to Netley in Hampshire before being sent, on the 25th of June, to a hospital specialising in shell-shock cases, Craiglockhart War Hospital in Edinburgh.

OWEN MEETS SASSOON AND HIS POETIC STYLE IS TRANSFORMED

Siegfried Sassoon had been sent to Craiglockhart on the 20th of July. On the 16th or 17th of August Owen called on Sassoon. Under his arm he carried several volumes of poetry, Sassoon's *The Old Huntsman*. He wanted Sassoon to autograph them.

It was the most important meeting of Owen's life. As a result of his conversations and friendship with Sassoon, Owen changed his poetic style and was stimulated into a burst of poetic activity. All his major poems were written in the next thirteen months.

Shortly after their first meeting Owen showed some of his war poems to Sassoon, probably including, *To a Comrade in Flanders*. (See page 151.) Although Sassoon considered Owen's poetry sickly sweet he recognised that Owen had talent and encouraged him to write in a more earthy style.

In one week, in October, he completed drafts of six poems, including *Disabled* and *Dulce et Decorum Est*.

THE SENTRY

We'd found an old Boche[1] dugout,[2] and he knew,
And gave us hell; for shell on frantic shell
Lit[3] full on top, but never quite burst through.

Rain, guttering down in waterfalls of slime,
Kept slush waist-high and rising hour by hour,
And choked the steps too thick with clay to climb.
What murk of air remained stank old, and sour
With fumes from whizz-bangs,[4] and the smell of men
Who'd lived there years, and left their curse in the den,
If not their corpses . . .

                          There we herded from the blast
Of whizz-bangs; but one found our door at last, –
Buffeting eyes and breath, snuffing[5] the candles,
And thud! Flump! Thud! Down the steep steps came thumping
And sploshing in the flood, deluging muck,
The sentry's body; then his rifle, handles
Of old Boche bombs, and mud in ruck on ruck.[6]
We dredged it[7] up, for dead, until he whined,
"O sir, my eyes – I'm blind – I'm blind – I'm blind."
Coaxing, I held a flame against his lids
And said if he could see the least blurred light
He was not blind; in time they'd get all right.
"I can't," he sobbed. Eyeballs, huge-bulged like squids',
Watch my dreams[8] still, – yet I forgot him[9] there
In posting[10] Next for duty, and sending a scout
To beg a stretcher somewhere, and flound'ring about
To other posts under the shrieking[11] air.

Those other wretches, how they bled and spewed,
And one who would have drowned[12] himself for good. –
I try not to remember these things now.
Let Dread hark back for one word only:[13] how,
Half-listening to that sentry's moans and jumps,
And the wild chattering of his shivered teeth,
Renewed most horribly whenever crumps[14]
Pummelled[15] the roof and slogged[16] the air beneath –
Through the dense din, I say, we heard him shout
"I see your lights!" – But ours had long gone out.

August? 1917 - September, 1918

For the background to this poem see Owen's letter of 16 January 1917.

1 German   2 *dugout* - roughly made room or cell, usually dug in the side of a trench   3 landed
4 *whizz-bangs* - shells which exploded instantly after you heard the "whizz" of their flight
5 putting-out   6 *ruck on ruck* - fold; like cloth folding as it is pushed along a smooth surface, fold
after fold spilling forwards   7 the body (for a moment the man was presumed dead)   8 *Watch my
dreams* - keep returning to look at me in my dreams   9 *I forgot him* - I had to leave him to get on
with the job   10 organising   11 the noise of the shells   12 *one who would have drowned himself* -
one man was in such despair that he thought of drowning himself   13 *Let Dread hark back for one
word only* - the sense of these words seems to be, let fear bring back memories of . . .   Owen was
working on this poem only a few weeks before his death and may have had some improving to do
14 the sound of explosions muffled by the mud the shells landed in   15 repeatedly beat upon
16 struck

ANTHEM[1] FOR DOOMED YOUTH

What passing-bells[2] for these who die as cattle?
Only the monstrous anger of the guns.
Only the stuttering rifles' rapid rattle
Can patter out[3] their hasty orisons.[4]
No mockeries[5] now for them; no prayers nor bells;
Nor any voice of mourning save the choirs, –
The shrill, demented[6] choirs of wailing shells;
And bugles[7] calling for them from sad shires.[8]

What candles[9] may be held to speed them all?
Not in the hands of boys but in their eyes
Shall shine the holy glimmers of goodbyes.
The pallor[10] of girls' brows shall be their pall;
Their flowers the tenderness of patient minds,
And each slow dusk[11] a drawing-down of blinds.[12]

September - October, 1917

1 perhaps best known in the expression "The National Anthem;" also, an important religious song
(often expressing joy); here, perhaps, a solemn song of celebration   2 *passing-bells* - a bell tolled
after someone's death to announce the death to the world   3 *patter out* - rapidly speak   4 prayers,
here funeral prayers   5 ceremonies which are insults. Here Owen seems to be suggesting that the
Christian religion, with its loving God, can have nothing to do with the deaths of so many thousands
of men   6 raving mad   7 a bugle is played at military funerals (sounding the last post)   8 English
counties and countryside from which so many of the soldiers came   9 church candles, or the
candles lit in the room where a body lies in a coffin   10 paleness   11 dusk has a symbolic
significance here   12 *drawing-down of blinds* - normally a preparation for night, but also, here, the
tradition of drawing the blinds in a room where a dead person lies, as a sign to the world and as a
mark of respect. The coming of night is like the drawing down of blinds.

DISABLED

He sat in a wheeled chair, waiting for dark,
And shivered in his ghastly suit of grey,
Legless, sewn short at elbow. Through the park
Voices of boys rang saddening like a hymn,
Voices of play and pleasure after day,
Till gathering sleep had mothered them from him.

About this time Town used to swing so gay
When glow-lamps budded in the light blue trees,
And girls glanced lovelier as the air grew dim, –
In the old times, before he threw away his knees.
Now he will never feel again how slim
Girls' waists are, or how warm their subtle hands.
All of them touch him like some queer disease.

There was an artist silly for his face,[1]
For it was younger[2] than his youth, last year.
Now, he is old; his back will never brace;[3]
He's lost his colour very far from here,
Poured it[4] down shell-holes till the veins ran dry,
And half his lifetime lapsed[5] in the hot race
And leap of purple[6] spurted from his thigh.

One time he liked a blood-smear down his leg,
After the matches, carried shoulder-high.
It was after football, when he'd drunk a peg,[7]
He thought he'd better join.   –   He wonders why.
Someone had said he'd look a god in kilts,[8]
That's why; and maybe, too, to please his Meg,
Aye, that was it, to please the giddy jilts[9]
He asked to join. He didn't have to beg;
Smiling they wrote his lie: aged nineteen[10] years.
Germans he scarcely thought of; all their guilt,[11]
And Austria's, did not move him. And no fears
Of Fear[12] came yet. He thought of jewelled hilts
For daggers in plaid socks; of smart salutes;
And care of arms; and leave; and pay arrears;
Esprit de corps;[13] and hints for young recruits.
And soon, he was drafted out with drums and cheers.

Some cheered him home, but not as crowds cheer Goal.
Only a solemn man who brought him fruits
Thanked him; and then enquired about his soul.

Now, he will spend a few sick years in institutes,
And do what things the rules consider wise,
And take whatever pity they may dole.
Tonight he noticed how the women's eyes
Passed from him to the strong men that were whole.
How cold and late it is! Why don't they come[14]
And put him into bed? Why don't they come?

October 1917 - July, 1918

1 *silly for his face* - ridiculously keen to do his portrait   2 *was younger* - appeared younger than he
really was   3 straighten, support   4 *Poured it* - poured his blood away   5 lost   6 dark, red blood
7 a quantity of alcoholic drink   8 he hoped to join a Scottish regiment and wear a kilt   9 *giddy jilts*
- silly girls who had no interest in him   10 *aged nineteen* - the minimum age for service at the
front was nineteen   11 *all their guilt* - he never considered all the wrong the Germans and Austrians
had done (the reason all supporters of the war believed the British should fight)   12 *fears of Fear* -
he wasn't worried about feeling afraid   13 *Esprit de corps* - sense of comradeship, friendship   14
Why don't they come? - as well as the obvious meaning, this has the extra one of referring to an old
recruiting poster showing a soldier waiting for reinforcements, with the slogan, "Will they never
come?" Recruiting was commonly done at football matches.

DULCE ET DECORUM EST[1]

Bent double, like old beggars under sacks,
Knock-kneed, coughing like hags, we cursed through sludge,
Till on the haunting flares[2] we turned our backs
And towards our distant rest[3] began to trudge.
Men marched asleep. Many had lost their boots
But limped on, blood-shod. All went lame; all blind;
Drunk with fatigue; deaf even to the hoots[4]
Of tired, outstripped[5] Five-Nines[6] that dropped behind.

Gas![7] Gas! Quick, boys! —   An ecstasy of fumbling,
Fitting the clumsy helmets[8] just in time;
But someone still was yelling out and stumbling,
And flound'ring like a man in fire or lime[9] . . .
Dim, through the misty panes[10] and thick green light,
As under a green sea, I saw him drowning.

In all my dreams, before my helpless sight,
He plunges at me, guttering,[11] choking, drowning.

If in some smothering dreams you too could pace
Behind the wagon that we flung him in,
And watch the white eyes writhing in his face,
His hanging face, like a devil's sick of sin;
If you could hear, at every jolt, the blood
Come gargling from the froth-corrupted lungs,
Obscene as cancer, bitter as the cud[12]
Of vile, incurable sores on innocent tongues,
My friend, you would not tell with such high zest[13]
To children ardent[14] for some desperate glory,
The old Lie; Dulce et Decorum est
Pro patria mori.[15]

8 October 1917 - March, 1918

1 *DULCE ET DECORUM EST* - the first words of a Latin saying (taken from an ode by Horace). The words were widely understood and often quoted at the start of the First World War. They mean "It is sweet and right." The full saying ends the poem: *Dulce et decorum est pro patria mori* - it is sweet and right to die for your country. In other words, it is a wonderful and great honour to fight and die for your country   2 rockets which were sent up to burn with a brilliant glare to light up men and other targets in the area between the front lines (See illustration, page 118.)   3 a camp away from the front line where exhausted soldiers might rest for a few days, or longer   4 the noise made by the shells rushing through the air   5 outpaced, the soldiers have struggled beyond the reach of these shells which are now falling behind them as they struggle away from the scene of battle   6 *Five-Nines* - 5.9 calibre explosive shells   7 poison gas. From the symptoms it would appear to be chlorine or phosgene gas. The filling of the lungs with fluid had the same effects as when a person drowned   8 the early name for gas masks   9 a white chalky substance which can burn live tissue   10 the glass in the eyepieces of the gas masks   11 Owen probably meant flickering out like a candle or gurgling like water draining down a gutter, referring to the sounds in the throat of the choking man, or it might be a sound partly like stuttering and partly like gurgling   12 normally the regurgitated grass that cows chew; here a similar looking material was issuing from the soldier's mouth   13 *high zest* - idealistic enthusiasm, keenly believing in the rightness of the idea   14 keen   15 see note 1

GREATER LOVE[1]

Red lips are not so red
As the stained stones kissed by the English dead.
Kindness of wooed[2] and wooer[3]
Seems shame to their love pure.
O Love, your eyes lose lure[4]
When I behold eyes blinded in my stead!

Your slender attitude
Trembles not exquisite like limbs knife-skewed,
Rolling and rolling there
Where God seems not to care;
Till the fierce Love they bear
Cramps them in death's extreme decrepitude.[5]

Your voice sings not so soft, –
Though even as wind murmuring through raftered loft, –
Your dear voice is not dear,
Gentle, and evening clear,
As theirs whom none now hear,
Now earth has stopped their piteous mouths that coughed.

Heart, you were never hot,
Nor large, nor full like hearts made great with shot;[6]
And though your hand be pale,
Paler are all which trail[7]
Your cross through flame and hail:
Weep, you may weep, for you may touch them not.

Written October 1917 - July, 1918

1 For an account of Owen's views on "greater love" and Christianity see his letter dated 16th May
1917   2 a person who is courted   3 suitor, a person courting, or going out with, another (the
wooed)   4 power to attract   5 collapse, state of being worn-out   6 *great with shot* - heavy with
lead shot   7 drag, also a military term which describes a way of carrying a rifle i.e holding the
barrel, allowing the butt to drop below horizontal

INSENSIBILITY

Happy are men who yet before they are killed
Can let their veins run cold,
Whom no compassion fleers[1]
Or makes their feet
Sore on the alleys cobbled[2] with their brothers.
The front line withers.
But they are troops who fade, not flowers,
For poets' tearful fooling:
Men, gaps for filling:[3]
Losses, who might have fought
Longer; but no one bothers.

And some cease feeling
Even themselves or for themselves.
Dullness best solves
The tease and doubt of shelling,
And Chance's strange arithmetic
Comes simpler than the reckoning of their shilling.[4]
They keep no check on armies' decimation.

Happy are these who lose imagination:
They have enough to carry with amunition.
Their spirit drags no pack.[5]
Their old wounds, save with cold, can not more ache.
Having seen all things red,

Their eyes are rid
Of the hurt of the colour of blood for ever.
And terror's first constriction[6] over,
Their hearts remain small-drawn.
Their senses in some scorching cautery[7] of battle
Now long since ironed,
Can laugh among the dying, unconcerned.

Happy the soldier home, with not a notion
How somewhere, every dawn, some men attack,
And many sighs are drained.
Happy the lad whose mind was never trained:
His days are worth forgetting more than not.
He sings along the march
Which we march taciturn, because of dusk,
The long, forlorn, relentless trend
From larger day to huger night.

We wise, who with a thought besmirch[8]
Blood over all our soul,
How should we see our task
But through his blunt and lashless eyes?
Alive, he is not vital overmuch;
Dying, not mortal overmuch;
Nor sad, nor proud,
Nor curious at all.
He cannot tell
Old men's placidity[9] from his.

But cursed are dullards[10] whom no cannon stuns,
That they should be as stones.
Wretched are they, and mean
With paucity that never was simplicity.
By choice they made themselves immune
To pity and whatever moans in man
Before the last sea and the hapless stars;
Whatever mourns when many leave these shores:
Whatever shares
The eternal reciprocity[11] of tears.

October? 1917 - January? 1918

1 sneers at, scoffs at   2 the cobblestones Owen refers to here are the skulls of dead soldiers. This is apparent from a sentence in a letter to his sister Mary, in March 1918. "They are dying again at Beaumont Hamel, which already in 1916 was cobbled with skulls."   3 *gaps for filling* - a well known recruiting poster showed a line of soldiers with one gap. In the gap was a placard saying, "This space is reserved for a fit man."   4 soldiers' pay   5 *drags no pack* - carries no burden, soldiers carried a heavy rucksack full of supplies, into battle   6 tightening of muscles with fear   7 a wound burnt with a hot iron, or chemical to encourage healing or prevent bleeding   8 smear, make dirty   9 calmness, stillness   10 stupid people   11 literally, giving and receiving, exchanging

On the 28th of October 1917 the Medical Board at Craiglockhart said
Owen was well enough to be returned to his unit in England to perform
light duties. He was sent on three weeks leave before joining the
Manchesters 5th (Reserve) Battalion in Scarborough towards the end of
November.

APOLOGIA PRO POEMATE MEO[1]

I, too, saw God through mud, –
The mud that cracked on cheeks when wretches smiled.
War brought more glory to their eyes than blood,
And gave their laughs more glee than shakes a child.

Merry it was to laugh there –
Where death becomes absurd and life absurder.
For power was on us as we slashed bones bare
Not to feel sickness or remorse of murder.

I, too, have dropped off Fear –
Behind the barrage,[2] dead as my platoon,[3]
And sailed my spirit surging light and clear
Past the entanglement[4] where hopes lay strewn;

And witnessed exultation –
Faces that used to curse me, scowl for scowl,
Shine and lift up with passion of oblation,[5]
Seraphic[6] for an hour; though they were foul.

I have made fellowships –
Untold of happy lovers in old song.
For love is not the binding of fair lips
With the soft silk of eyes that look and long,

By Joy, whose ribbon slips, –
But wound with war's hard wire whose stakes are strong;
Bound with the bandage of the arm that drips;
Knit in the webbing of the rifle-thong.

I have perceived much beauty
In the hoarse oaths that kept our courage straight;
Heard music in the silentness of duty;
Found peace where shell-storms spouted reddest spate.

Nevertheless, except you[7] share
With them in hell the sorrowful dark of hell,
Whose world is but the trembling of a flare
And heaven but as the highway for a shell,

You shall not hear their mirth:
You shall not come to think them well content
By any jest of mine. These men are worth
Your tears. You are not worth their merriment.

November, December, 1917

1 *APOLOGIA PRO POEMATE MEO* – Justification for my poetry 2 the continuous firing of
shells from a long line of field guns 3 *dead as my platoon* - hardened, uncaring, insensible as his
platoon to the terror of the situation 4 barbed wire entanglements set up to protect trenches against
enemy troops 5 making a religious offering 6 angels 7 the ignorant, uncaring civilians back home

THE SHOW[1]

We have fallen in the dreams the ever living
Breathe on the tarnished mirror of the world,
And then smooth out with ivory hands and sigh.*
                                    – W B Yeats

My soul looked down from a vague height, with Death,
As unremembering how I rose or why,
And saw a sad land, weak with sweats of dearth,[2]
Gray, cratered like the moon with hollow woe,
And pitted with great pocks[3] and scabs of plagues.

Across its beard, that horror of harsh wire,
There moved thin caterpillars, slowly uncoiled.
It seemed they pushed themselves to be as plugs
Of ditches, where they writhed and shrivelled, killed.

By them had slimy paths been trailed and scraped
Round myriad[4] warts that might be little hills.

From gloom's last dregs these long-strung creatures[5] crept,
And vanished out of dawn down hidden holes.

(And smell came up from those foul openings
As out of mouths, or deep wounds deepening.)

On dithering feet upgathered, more and more,
Brown[6] strings, towards strings of grey,[7] with bristling spines,[8]
All migrants from green fields, intent on mire.

Those that were grey, of more abundant spawns,[9]
Ramped[10] on the rest and ate them and were eaten.

I saw their bitten backs curve, loop, and straighten.
I watched those agonies curl, lift, and flatten.

Whereat, in terror what that sight might mean,
I reeled and shivered earthward like a feather.

And Death fell with me, like a deepening moan.
And He, picking a manner of worm,[11] which half had hid
Its bruises in the earth, but crawled no further,
Showed me its feet, the feet of many men,
And the fresh-severed head of it, my head.[12]

November 1917 - May, 1918

For the background to this poem see Owen's letters of 19th February
and 14th May 1917.

* Owen misquotes Yeats who wrote, "burnished mirror."
1 an expression commonly used by soldiers meaning battle   2 famine, want, scarcity, barrenness;
perhaps the last of these meanings makes the most sense here   3 spots (raised spots on the skin,
full of puss, as in smallpox)   4 an immense number   5 *long-strung creatures* - a line of soldiers
which seen from a great height might seem like a single creature   6 the khaki British uniform
7 the colour of German uniforms   8 *bristling spines* - rifles with bayonets attached   9 a
contemptuous term for offspring; literally, a mass of eggs laid in water or the dust-like seeds of
mushrooms or toadstools   10 piled up   11 *a manner of worm* - by Owen's description of it (having
feet) he clearly means a caterpillar, and may be using the word 'worm' partly because of associated
ideas and partly for its more unpleasantly expressive sound. The caterpillars of the poem may be
maggots. Owen would no doubt have seen these in rotting, stinking flesh   12 *the fresh-severed
head of it, my head* - Owen would have been the "head" of a line of soldiers on occasions when he,
as a commanding officer, had led his platoon of soldiers in single file.

In the extraordinary cold of early 1917 soldiers suffered terribly from frostbite, bronchitis, and severe
rheumatism. Many died of exposure.

DECLARED FIT FOR THE FRONT LINE

In March 1918 Owen was transferred to the army base in Ripon,
Yorkshire. He was passed fit for general service on the 4th of June
and rejoined the 5th Manchesters at Scarborough the next day. He was
declared fit for front line service on 26th August.

EXPOSURE

Our brains ache, in the merciless iced east winds that knive us . . .
Wearied we keep awake because the night is silent . . .
Low, drooping flares confuse our memory of the salient . . .[1]
Worried by silence, sentries whisper, curious, nervous,
    But nothing happens.

Watching, we hear the mad gusts tugging on the wire,
Like twitching agonies of men among its brambles.
Northward, incessantly, the flickering gunnery rumbles,
Far off, like a dull rumour of some other war.
    What are we doing here?

The poignant misery of dawn begins to grow . . .
We only know war lasts, rain soaks, and clouds sag stormy.
Dawn massing in the east her melancholy army
Attacks once more in ranks on shivering ranks of grey,[2]
    But nothing happens.

Sudden successive flights of bullets streak the silence.
Less deathly than the air that shudders black with snow,
With sidelong flowing flakes that flock, pause, and renew;
We watch them wandering up and down the wind's nonchalance,[3]
    But nothing happens.

Pale flakes with fingering stealth come feeling for our faces.
We cringe[4] in holes, back on forgotten dreams, and stare, snow-dazed,
Deep into grassier ditches. So we drowse, sun-dozed,[5]
Littered with blossoms[6] trickling where the blackbird fusses.
    Is it that we are dying?

Slowly our ghosts[7] drag home: glimpsing the sunk fires, glozed[8]
With crusted dark-red jewels; crickets jingle there;
For hours the innocent mice rejoice: the house is theirs;
Shutters and doors, all closed; on us the doors are closed.
    We turn back to our dying.

Since we believe not otherwise can kind fires burn;
Nor ever suns smile true on child, or field, or fruit.
For God's invincible spring our love is made afraid;
Therefore, not loath, we lie out here; therefore were born,
    For love of God seems dying.[9]

Tonight, this frost will fasten on this mud and us,
Shrivelling many hands, puckering foreheads crisp.[10]
The burying-party, picks and shovels in shaking grasp,
Pause over half-known faces. All their eyes are ice,
    But nothing happens.

December 1917 - September, 1918

For the background to this poem see Owen's letter of 4th February 1917.

1 trenches jutting forward from the front line   2 grey like the colour of the German uniforms
3 indifference, the snowflakes wander in the wind not caring where they go   4 cower, huddle up,
curl up in fear   5 *sun-dozed* - able to sleep because the sun is now warming them   6 the
snow-flakes   7 the soldiers imagine themselves as ghosts going wearily home   8 glowing and
glazed   9 *For love of God seems dying* - the soldiers are prepared to die for the love of God and
the protection of the other things mentioned in this verse 10 frozen (perhaps to death)

STRANGE MEETING

It seemed that out of battle I escaped
Down some profound dull tunnel, long since scooped
Through granites which titanic[1] wars had groined.[2]

Yet also there encumbered sleepers groaned,
Too fast in thought or death to be bestirred.
Then, as I probed them, one sprang up, and stared
With piteous recognition in fixed eyes,
Lifting distressful hands, as if to bless.
And by his smile, I knew that sullen hall;
By his dead smile I knew we stood in Hell.

With a thousand pains that vision's face was grained;[3]
Yet no blood reached there from the upper ground,
And no guns thumped, or down the flues made moan.
"Strange friend," I said, "here is no cause to mourn."
"None," said that other, "save the undone[4] years,
The hopelessness. Whatever hope is yours,
Was my life also; I went hunting wild
After the wildest beauty in the world,
Which lies not calm in eyes, or braided hair,
But mocks the steady running of the hour,
And if it grieves, grieves richlier than here.

For by my glee might many men have laughed,
And of my weeping something had been[5] left,
Which must die now. I mean the truth untold,
The pity of war, the pity war distilled.
Now men will go content with what we spoiled,
Or, discontent, boil bloody, and be spilled.
They will be swift with swiftness of the tigress.
None will break ranks,[6] though nations trek from progress.
Courage was mine, and I had mystery,
Wisdom was mine, and I had mastery:
To miss the march of this retreating world
Into vain citadels[7] that are not walled.
Then, when much blood had clogged their chariot-wheels,
I would go up and wash them from sweet wells,
Even with truths that lie too deep for taint.
I would have poured my spirit without stint
But not through wounds; not on the cess of war.
Foreheads of men have bled where no wounds were.

I am the enemy you killed, my friend.
I knew you in this dark; for so you frowned
Yesterday through me as you jabbed and killed.
I parried; but my hands were loath and cold.
Let us sleep now . . .”

January - March, 1918 (From earlier fragments)

1 huge-scale   2 hollowed   3 marked, lined   4 unlived   5 *had been* - might have been   6 *break
ranks* - take a stand against the actions of the many   7 *vain citadels* - literally arrogant cities, but
implying arrogant or dictatorial nations

THE SEND-OFF

Down the close darkening lanes they sang their way
To the siding-shed,[1]
And lined the train with faces grimly gay.

Their breasts were stuck all white with wreath and spray
As men's are, dead.

Dull porters watched them, and a casual tramp
Stood staring hard,
Sorry to miss them from the upland camp.

Then, unmoved, signals nodded, and a lamp
Winked to the guard.

So secretly, like wrongs hushed-up, they went.
They were not ours:
We never heard to which front these were sent;

Nor there if they yet mock what women meant
Who gave them flowers.

Shall they return to beating of great bells
In wild train-loads?
A few, a few, too few for drums[2] and yells,[3]
May creep back, silent, to village wells,
Up half-known roads.

April - July, 1918

1 *siding shed* - a shed by or over a siding (a short stretch of railway line branching off a main line)
2 drums of a military band celebrating their return   3 the cheer and shouts of the crowd

FUTILITY[1]

Move him into the sun –
Gently its touch awoke him once,
At home, whispering of fields unsown.
Always it woke him, even in France,
Until this morning and this snow.
If anything might rouse him now
The kind old sun will know.

Think how it wakes the seeds –
Woke, once, the clays of a cold star.[2]
Are limbs, so dear achieved, are sides
Full-nerved – still warm – too hard to stir?
Was it for this the clay grew tall?[3]
O what made fatuous sunbeams toil
To break earth's sleep at all?

May, 1918

1 a waste of time, uselessness, pointlessness   2 *Woke, once, the clays of a cold star* - Owen is
referring to the idea expressed in the Bible that man is made out of clay. "Thou hast made me of
clay and wilt thou bring me unto dust again?" (Job 10 v 9) – "And the Lord God formed man of
the dust of the ground." (Genesis 2 v 7)

MENTAL CASES

Who are these? Why sit they here in twilight?
Wherefore rock they, purgatorial shadows,[1]
Drooping tongues from jaws that slob their relish,[2]
Baring teeth that leer[3] like skulls' teeth wicked?[4]
Stroke on stroke of pain, – but what slow panic,
Gouged[5] these chasms[6] round their fretted sockets?[7]
Ever from their hair and through their hands' palms
Misery swelters.[8] Surely we have perished
Sleeping, and walk hell; but who these hellish?

– These are men whose minds the Dead have ravished.[9]
Memory fingers in their hair of murders,
Multitudinous[10] murders they once witnessed.
Wading sloughs[11] of flesh these helpless wander,
Treading blood from lungs that had loved laughter.
Always they must see these things and hear them,
Batter of guns and shatter of flying muscles,
Carnage incomparable,[12] and human squander[13]
Rucked[14] too thick for these men's extrication.[15]

Therefore still their eyeballs shrink tormented
Back into their brains, because on their sense
Sunlight seems a blood-smear; night comes blood-black;
Dawn breaks open like a wound that bleeds afresh.
– Thus their heads wear this hilarious, hideous,
Awful falseness of set-smiling corpses.

– Thus their hands are plucking at each other;
Picking at the rope-knouts[16] of their scourging;[17]
Snatching after us who smote[18] them, brother,
Pawing us who dealt them war and madness.

May-July, 1918

1 *purgatorial shadows* - shadows like those in purgatory (the place where souls go after death to be purified from sin)   2 *slob their relish* - let the food they are greatly enjoying dribble out of their mouths   3 look slyly or with obvious sexual desire   4 *skull's teeth wicked* - wicked looking teeth of skulls   5 hacked or chiselled   6 great cracks in the earth's surface   7 *fretted sockets* - the sockets are the hollows in which the eyes rest. Fretted means worn or cut, but the word 'fret' can also mean to worry   8 sweats as in a fever or oppressive heat   9 violently seized or carried away   10 a great many. Owen is here clearly referring to a scene in *Macbeth* where the expression *"multitudinous murders"* occurs (Act II, Scene 2). In this scene Macbeth is filled with intense fear, guilt, and shock because of the crime he has just committed.   11 marshland of deep sinking mud   12 *Carnage incomparable* - slaughter, with which there is nothing to compare   13 waste   14 piled up   15 disentangling, escape   16 *rope-knouts* - rope whips   17 severe whipping   18 struck, hit

Mental breakdown in the First World War is described on pages 105-106. Owen would have been all too familiar with the conditions of shell shock through personal experience and through meeting men in Craiglockhart War Hospital whose minds had been ruined for ever. This poem also seems to owe something to a passage in the Bible that Owen was probably familiar with: Revelations, chapter 7, verses 13-14. "What are these which are arrayed in white robes? And whence came they? And I said unto him, Sir, thou knowest . . . And he said unto me, These are they which came out of great tribulation, and have washed their robes, and made them white in the blood."

RETURNS TO FRANCE

Owen arrived in France on the 31st of August and reported to base camp at Etaples. By the 13th of September he had joined the Manchesters close to the front near Amiens and was soon in action as the Germans were driven swiftly back towards the Belgian border.

SPRING OFFENSIVE

Halted against the shade of a last hill,
They fed, and lying easy, were at ease;
And, leaning on the nearest chests or knees
Carelessly slept.
            But many there stood still
To face the stark, blank sky beyond the ridge,
Knowing their feet had come to the end of the world.

Marvelling they stood, and watched the long grass swirled
By the May breeze, murmurous with wasp and midge;
And though the summer oozed into their veins
Like an injected drug for their bodies' pains,
Sharp on their souls hung the imminent ridge of grass;
Fearfully flashed the sky's mysterious glass.

Hour after hour they ponder the warm field –
And the far valley behind, where buttercups
Had blessed with gold[1] their slow boots coming up;
When even the little brambles would not yield,
But clutched and clung to them like sorrowing arms;
They breathe like trees unstirred.

Till like a cold gust thrills the little word
At which each body and its soul begird[2]
And tighten them for battle. No alarms[3]
Of bugles, no high flags, no clamorous haste –
Only a lift and flare[4] of eyes that faced
The sun, like a friend with whom their love is done.
O larger shone that smile against the sun –
Mightier than his whose bounty these have spurned.

So, soon they topped the hill, and raced together
Over an open stretch of herb and heather
Exposed. And instantly the whole sky burned
With fury against them; earth set sudden cups[5]
In thousands for their blood; and the green slope
Chasmed and deepened sheer to infinite space.

Of them who running on that last high place
Breasted the surf of bullets, or went up
On the hot blast and fury of hell's upsurge,
Or plunged and fell away past this world's verge,[6]
Some say God caught them even before they fell.[7]

But what say such as from existence' brink
Ventured[8] but drave[9] too swift to sink,
The few who rushed in the body to enter hell,
And there out-fiending all its fiends[10] and flames
With superhuman inhumanities,[11]
Long-famous glories,[12] immemorial[13] shames[14] –
And crawling slowly back, have by degrees
Regained cool peaceful air in wonder –
Why speak not they of comrades that went under?

July - late September, 1918

1 *blessed with gold* - the idea is that the pollen or petals of buttercups had coloured boots gold as the soldiers walked (This is virtually impossible in practice.) 2 put on battle gear 3 signals, announcements (of the time to advance) 4 shine, opening in surprise or fear 5 *set sudden cups* - the shell craters suddenly created by the arriving shells, but also suggesting, perhaps, sacrificial chalices 6 edge 7 fell in battle (died) 8 dared to go forward 9 drove, rushed 10 *out-fiending all its fiends* - committing atrocities worse than all the devils (fiends) in hell 11 crimes against the human race 12 much praised battles or heroic deeds 13 immemorial usually means ancient beyond memory. Here, the idea may be (as with "long-famous") projected into the future and mean to be remembered over many centuries. 14 disgraceful actions

Spring Offensive is one of the last poems Owen wrote. See his letter of 14th May 1917 (page 155) for an account of the experience on which this poem is based.

SMILE, SMILE, SMILE

Head to limp head, the sunk-eyed wounded scanned
Yesterday's *Mail*; the casualties (typed small)
And (large) Vast Booty from our Latest Haul.
Also, they read of Cheap Homes, not yet planned,
"For," said the paper, "when this war is done
The men's first instincts will be making homes.
Meanwhile their foremost need is aerodromes,
It being certain war has but begun.
Peace would do wrong to our undying dead.
The sons we offered might regret they died
If we got nothing lasting in their stead.
We must be solidly indemnified.
Though all be worthy Victory which all bought,
We rulers sitting in this ancient spot
Would wrong our very selves if we forgot
The greatest glory will be theirs who fought,
Who kept this nation in integrity."[1]
Nation? – The half-limbed readers did not chafe[2]
But smiled at one another curiously
Like secret men who know their secret safe.
(This is the thing they know and never speak,
That England one by one had fled to France,
Not many elsewhere now, save under France.)
Pictures of these broad smiles appear each week,
And people in whose voice real feeling rings
Say: How they smile! They're happy now, poor things.

Late September, 1918

1 *in integrity* - whole, complete   2 argue against the idea

Smile, Smile, Smile was inspired by articles in the *Daily Mail* and *The Times* which Owen's mother had sent him.

OWEN'S LAST DAYS

Owen in fierce fighting wins the Military Cross for his daring and success

Late afternoon on 1st October, and on through the night, the 96th Brigade of the Manchesters went into action near the villages of Joncourt and Sequehart, six miles north of St Quentin. There was "savage hand-to- hand fighting." At first the Germans were driven back, but they made repeated counter-attacks. Owen threw himself into his task. He wrote to his mother, telling her how he had captured a German Machine Gun and scores of prisoners . . . He said he only shot one man with his revolver.

Showing his usual concern for his mother's feelings he gave the impression that he had killed only one man, but the citation accompanying the Military Cross which he was awarded for his actions that night make it clear that he used the machine gun to kill a large number of men. "He personally manipulated a captured machine gun in an isolated position and inflicted considerable losses on the enemy. Throughout he behaved most gallantly."

Owen's last letter

Owen knew that the war was nearing its end. The Germans were in full retreat. The British soldiers were welcomed with joyful gratitude by the French, and he was really enjoying himself being part of a band of soldiers. In his last letter to his mother, written on 31st October, he describes the maty atmosphere in his billets, "The Smoky Cellar of Forester's House."

> It is a great life. I am more oblivious than alas! yourself, dear Mother, of the ghastly glimmering of the guns outside, and the hollow crashing of the shells.

> There is no danger down here, or if any, it will be well over before you read these lines.

> I hope you are as warm as I am; as serene in your room as I am here . . . Of this I am certain: you could not be visited by a band of friends half so fine as surround me here.

> Ever Wilfred x

On 4th November 1918 the Manchesters were ordered into action in the early hours. The aim was to cross the Sambre Canal just south of the little village of Ors, not far from the Belgian border. The Germans with their machine gunners held the south bank. At 5.45 am Owen's platoon started to attempt the crossing with floats and rafts. Wilfred Owen, standing at the water's edge, was encouraging his men when he was hit and killed.

Seven days later the war was over. Church bells rang throughout the country. As they were ringing in Shrewsbury, Susan and Tom Owen received the telegram announcing their son's death.

The grave stone of Wilfred Owen in the village cemetery at Ors, in north eastern France.

Owen's mother paid for the addition of words from his poem, *The End.* However, she missed the question mark at the end of the second sentence and so reversed her son's original meaning. See the text of his poem on page 152.

COMMENTS ON THE POETRY OF WILFRED OWEN

At the time of his death Owen was unknown to the general public, only five of his poems having been published in his lifetime. When more of his work began to be published, popular writers said it was worthless. It was many years before he became recognised as a great poet. His fellow war poets were the first to appreciate Owen's talent.

Sir Henry Newbolt on Owen

> Owen, and the rest of the broken men who rail at the old men who sent the young to die: they suffered cruelly, but in the nerves and not in the heart. – They haven't the experience or the imagination to know the extreme of human agony . . . I don't think these shell-shocked war poems will move our grandchildren greatly – there's nothing fundamental or final about them.

Sir Henry Newbolt, letter to Lady Hylton, 2 August, 1924.

W B Yeats on Owen

Wilfred Owen I consider unworthy of the poet's corner of a
country newspaper . . . He is all blood, dirt and sucked sugar
stick . . .

W B Yeats, letter to Dorothy Wellesley, 21 December, 1936.

I have a distaste for certain poems written in the midst of the great
war; they are in all the anthologies . . . I have rejected these
poems . . . passive suffering is not a theme for poetry.

W B Yeats,
Introduction to *The Oxford Book of Modern Verse*, 1936.

Siegfried Sassoon on Owen

This verse with its sumptuous epithets and large-scale imagery,
its noble naturalness and the depth of meaning, had impressive
affinities with Keats, whom he took as his supreme exemplar.

I can only affirm that he was a man of absolute integrity of mind.
He never wrote his poems (as so many war poets did) to make the
effect of a personal gesture. He pitied others; he did not pity
himself.

Edmund Blunden on Owen

No poet has so utterly grasped the terror of particular moments. . .
He is first and foremost the witness of the war's effect on the spirit
of man.

In Owen we lost a poet of rare force . We have hinted at the spirit
of his verse; the letter is as masterly. The very make of his
language is hard and remorseless or strange and sombre as he
wills.

Dominic Hibberd on Owen

Few poems adopt a preaching tone: more often, Owen involves
himself, sometimes at the very end of the poem, or leaves the
reader to make up his own mind, closing several poems with a
question mark. These poems that do preach a moral directly at
the reader seem less fluent than the rest.

Although he classified a number of his poems as Protest, Owen is
not a poet of protest: the war was a human catastrophe and he
himself as a human, an officer and a poet, was part of it. It was
this wider sympathy and more accurate self-knowledge that was
to make him a much greater poet than Sassoon.

14

THE END OF THE WAR

The end of the war was met with relief, jubilation and partying by many, but others felt only physical and mental exhaustion, heartbreak, and loss.

BETRAYAL

At the end of the war Vera Brittain was close to mental collapse. She had endured the exhausting and traumatic experience of working in military hospitals. She had suffered the loss of a close friend, her fiancé and her brother.

HOSPITAL SANCTUARY

When you have lost your all in a world's upheaval,
Suffered and prayed, and found your prayers were vain,
When love is dead, and hope has no renewal –
These need you still; come back to them again.

When the sad days bring you the loss of all ambition,
And pride is gone that gave you strength to bear,
When dreams are shattered, and broken is all decision -
Turn you to these, dependent on your care.

They too have fathomed the depths of human anguish,
Seen all that counted flung like chaff away;
The dim abodes of pain wherein they languish
Offer that peace for which at last you pray.

Vera Brittain, September, 1918

Although the war was over Britain continued to blockade German ports to stop food supplies from getting through. The population had been reduced to eating dogs and cats. Tens of thousands starved to death. The aim of the Allies was to ensure that Germany would accept crippling terms in the treaties which would eventually be signed.

In the treaty negotiations after the war the enormous payments demanded from Germany by the victorious countries seemed to Vera Brittain to be unjust. She believed it was not the kind of victory that

justified the lost lives of the young men she had loved. She could not
bear to read the details of the peace treaty. She wrote:

> I was beginning already to suspect that my generation had been
> deceived, its young courage cynically exploited, its idealism
> betrayed, and I did not want to know the details of that betrayal.

A DEAD STATESMAN

I could not dig: I dared not rob:
Therefore I lied to please the mob.
Now all my lies are proved untrue
And I must face the men I slew.
What tale shall serve me here among
Mine angry and defrauded young?

Rudyard Kipling

COMMON FORM

If any question why we died,
Tell them, because our fathers lied.[1]

Rudyard Kipling

1 *fathers lied* - possibly a comment on politicians who urged young men to fight. Dominic
Hibberd suggests that the statesmen who lied were the ones who failed to build Britain's armies
and military resources before the war. Another possibility is that Kipling may have been blaming
himself for encouraging young men to fight and for the death of his only son in the war

THE GLORIOUS ARMY

FOR A WAR MEMORIAL
Clifton College, 1914 - 1918

From the Great Marshal[1] to the last recruit
These, Clifton, were thyself, thy spirit in deed,
Thy flower of chivalry,[2] thy fallen fruit
And thine immortal seed.

Henry Newbolt

1 *Great Marshal* - Haig, a former student at Clifton College. 2 *flower of chivalry* - best example
of courage and honour

So great was the gratitude and admiration for the work of Field Marshal Haig after the war that Parliament made him an Earl, and voted him a gift of £100,000.

England's most popular civilian poet at the time of the war was inspired to Baldrickian heights in his resounding celebration of the war's end, a thirty-two page poem, *All Clear!*   Here is a short extract.

ALL CLEAR!

... Right willingly they died,
Right joyfully they live,
For ever by Thy side,
Since Thou dost honour give. . .

All Clear! All Clear!
The evil days are gone,
The Prince of Peace is here
To claim His Throne.
All Clear! All Clear!
The evil days are gone. . .

John Oxenham

MISGIVINGS

Lloyd George's warning

Representatives of the warring nations met at the palace of Versailles, a few miles south of Paris, to discuss peace terms. Lloyd George warned that penalties which were harsh would create a seething anger in the German people which would make them want to start another war as soon as they were able. Popular newspapers in Britain called for outrageous penalties. The terms of the Versailles Treaty did not satisfy Britain's newspapers, but they were harsh enough to have the effect predicted by Lloyd George.

NIGHTFALL

Hooded in angry mist, the sun goes down:
Steel-grey the clouds roll out across the sea:
Is this a kingdom? Then give Death the crown,
For here no emperor hath won, save He.

Herbert Asquith

NOTES ON SOME FIRST WORLD WAR POETS

HAROLD BEGBIE, 1871-1929.

Journalist and verse writer. Sent by the *Daily Chronicle* to America in 1914 to speak on the British view of the war.

LAURENCE BINYON, 1869-1943.

Poet and Art Historian, born in Lancaster. He worked in the British Museum for forty years from 1893 with a brief spell in France working as a stretcher-bearer. His famous poem, *For the Fallen,* was written in the first weeks of the war. It is quoted every year in Remembrance Day Celebrations throughout Britain.

EDMUND BLUNDEN, 1896-1974.

Born in Yalding, Kent and educated at Christ's Hospital (school). Volunteered at the age of 17. He was awarded the Military Cross. The majority of Blunden's war poems were written in the 1920's. He promoted interest in Wilfred Owen's poems.

ROBERT SEYMOUR BRIDGES, 1844-1930.

Poet, dramatist and critic, born in Walmer, Kent. He practiced as a doctor until he was thirty-seven. He became Poet Laureate in 1913. In September 1914 he wrote a letter to *The Times* justifying the war as a "holy war" a "fight of good against evil".

VERA MARY BRITTAIN, 1893-1970.

Born in Newcastle under Lyme, Staffordshire, and grew up in Macclesfield and Buxton. Her *Testament of Youth* is one of the outstanding biographies of the First World War. She felt compelled to play a part, and worked as a voluntary nurse in England, France (where her first task was looking after wounded German prisoners) and Malta. She was moved to the verge of a nervous breakdown by her experiences in the war and the loss of a close friend, her fiancé and brother. She wrote her *Testament of Youth* to record the effect of the war on her generation. Her interest in politics sprang from a desire to understand the causes of the war which, in turn, she hoped

might help to prevent a recurrence of such a human catastrophe.

RUPERT CHAWNER BROOKE, 1887-1915.

Georgian poet. Born at Rugby. Educated at Rugby School and King's College, Cambridge. He was an atheist and active Socialist. He was a friend of Edward Marsh and worked with him to prepare and promote the first *Georgian Anthology* of poetry. After travelling in Germany, and, following his nervous breakdown he went on a world tour to recuperate. After hesitation about what course of action to take at the start of the First World War he joined the navy. He was a witness at the siege of Antwerp before writing his famous set of five sonnets called, *1914.* Though he had seen the devastation and suffering created by the war he kept it all at an emotional distance from himself, denying the realities of war. He had a deeply confused personality – given to both ecstatic enthusiasm and suicidal doubt. Following a mosquito bite he died of acute blood poisoning on board ship on his way to Gallipoli, and was buried on the Greek Island of Skyros.

MARY POSTGATE COLE, 1893-1980.

Socialist writer on politics. Author of detective novels.

ELEANOR FARJEON, 1881-1965.

Born in London. Well known as an author of children's stories. She was a close personal friend of Helen and Edward Thomas in the last few years of his life.

IVOR GURNEY, 1890-1937.

Born in Gloucester. Educated at King's School Gloucester and the Royal College of Music. He wrote poetry and music from before the war. He volunteered to fight and was initially turned down because of his poor eyesight. He was gassed and wounded and returned to Britain. Mental illness developed. He was diagnosed as a paranoid schizophrenic in 1922. He was committed to mental hospital where he was terrified by the electric shock treatment he was given. He continued to write poetry and compose – sometimes believing that he was still taking part in the war. He died of tuberculosis.

THOMAS HARDY, 1840-1928.

Born at Higher-Bockhampton near Dorchester. Educated at a private school in Dorchester. His pre-war poetry was admired by Sassoon. Best known as a classic novelist. He staunchly supported the war until it was over. A member of the Fight for Right Movement and worker for the Secret Bureau for Propaganda.

RUDYARD KIPLING, 1865-1936.

Born in Bombay. As a small child he was sent to England (Southsea) to be educated. Before the war he favoured re-armament. He was vigorous in his opposition to Germany. After his only son was killed in the Battle of the Loos, in September 1915, Kipling was heartbroken and his attitude to war changed. He is best known for his classic children's books. He was awarded the Nobel Prize for Literature in 1907. During the First World War he was Director of Propaganda to the British Colonies.

WINIFRED M LETTS, 1882-1971.

Born in Ireland. Worked as a Voluntary Aid Detachment nurse in England during the war.

EDITH NESBIT, 1858-1924.

Born in London. Socialist and writer of children's stories.

HENRY NEWBOLT, SIR, 1862-1924.

Born in Bilston, Staffordshire. Educated at Clifton College, Bristol and Corpus Christi College, Oxford. Barrister, then best selling poet. Establishment literary figure.

WILFRED EDWARD SALTER OWEN, 1893 -1918.

Born Oswestry, Shropshire. Educated at Birkenhead Institute and Shrewsbury Technical College. From the age of nineteen Owen wanted to be a poet and immersed himself in poetry, being especially impressed by Keats and Shelley. He was deeply attached to his mother to whom most of his 664 letters are addressed. (She saved every one.) He was a committed Christian and became lay assistant to the vicar of Dunsden near Reading 1911-1913. From 1913 to 1915 he worked as a language tutor in France. When war broke out he considered that he was more use to his country alive than dead.

Eventually, however, he felt pressured by the propaganda to become a soldier and volunteered on 21st October 1915. He spent just over a year training and arrived in France on the last day of 1916. He was full of boyish high spirits at being a soldier. Within a week he was experiencing the horror of war. It was a profound shock for him. "The people of England needn't hope. They must agitate," he wrote home.

He escaped bullets until the last week of the war, but he saw a good deal of front-line action: he was blown up, concussed and suffered shell-shock. He was sent to Craiglockhart, the psychiatric hospital in Edinburgh. All his major poems were written after he met Sassoon there. He was sent back to the trenches in September, 1918 and in October won the Military Cross by seizing a German machine-gun and using it to kill a number of Germans. On 4th November he was shot and killed near the village of Ors. The news of his death reached his parents home as the Armistice bells were ringing on 11th November.

JOHN OXENHAM, 1852-1941.

Popular novelist and poet. During the First World War his poetry sold over a million volumes, showing him to be the most popular poet at that time. His hymn, *For the Men at the Front*, was reputed to have sold eight million copies.

JESSIE POPE, 1868-1941.

Born in Leicester. Popular journalist and versifier. Regular contributor to *Punch*, *The Daily Mail*, and *The Daily Express*. Owen originally addressed *Dulce et Decorum Est* to her.

ISAAC ROSENBERG, 1890-1918.

Born in Bristol and educated in London's East End and the Slade School of Art. He was an artist and engraver as well as a poet, but finding no work he volunteered in October 1915. Killed 1st April 1918.

SIEGFRIED LORRAINE SASSOON, 1886-1967.

Born in Kent. Educated at Marlborough, and Clare College, Cambridge. He was a keen sportsman, loving cricket and foxhunting. He was the first war poet to volunteer – 3rd August 1914. Disillusion set in slowly. His first critical poem, *In the Pink*, was written in February 1916. He was the only English disillusioned First World War poet who made an effort to be politically effective.

As a captain in the Royal Welch fusiliers he became wildly angry at the death of one of his friends and fought recklessly, winning the Military Cross. He was wounded in the shoulder and later was shot in the head accidentally by one of his own men. The wound was a graze, but serious enough to put him out of the action for good from July 1918. It was when convalescing from his shoulder wound in the summer of 1917 that he made his famous protest about the war. As a result of this he was sent to Craiglockhart War Hospital in Edinburgh. There he met and encouraged Wilfred Owen with his poetry. He began to feel guilty about not fighting alongside his old comrades and returned to active service in November 1917.

He was the first to edit an edition of Wilfred Owen's poems. He married and had one son. He became a Roman Catholic in 1957.

ALAN SEEGER, 1888-1916.

Born in New York. Educated at Harvard. After graduating he lived in Greenwich Village for two years by sponging off his friends. He was aimless, anti-social and scruffy. His parents sent him to continue his studies in Paris. He saw the war as a liberation from the dullness of everyday life. On its outbreak he rushed to join the French Foreign Legion. He dreamed of leading heroic charges in the thick of battle. He was killed at Belloy-en-Santerre on the fourth day of the Battle of the Somme, 4th July, 1916.

CHARLES HAMILTON SORLEY, 1895-1915.

Born in Aberdeen. Educated at Marlborough, University College, Oxford, and for six months in Germany. He loved Germany and hated the idea of fighting for England. He was aware of how he was pressured into joining the army and resented it. He enlisted with the Suffolk Regiment. Promoted to Captain in August 1915 and killed in the Battle of Loos, 13th October 1915, at the age of twenty.

EDWARD THOMAS, 1878-1917.

He was born in London and educated at St Paul's School, and Lincoln College, Oxford. His first book was published when he was eighteen and in the next eighteen years he wrote over 30 books and thousands of articles and reviews. He was a friend of the American poet, Robert Frost. It was Frost who encouraged Thomas to write poetry. Starting in December 1914 and finishing in December 1916 Thomas wrote 144 poems – mainly about the English countryside, weather, the seasons – all of them written in England, in a straight, unadorned style – a number of them darkly influenced by the war. His poetry was rejected as fast as it was submitted to newspapers and periodicals, using his pseudonym, Edward Eastaway. He was a shy, self-effacing man who suffered from depression and came close to suicide. Having volunteered for the front, after eighteen months training, he went to France with the Royal Garrison Artillery at the end of January 1917. He was killed ten weeks later, on 9th April, leaving a wife and three children.

KATHARINE TYNAN, 1861-1931.

Born in Clondalkin, County Dublin. Educated Siena Convent, Drogheda. During the war she had a son serving in Palestine and another in France.

ROBERT ERNEST VERNÈDE, 1875-1917.

Educated at St Paul's School and St John's College, Oxford. Volunteered in September 1914. Wounded, invalided home. Although offered a safe job in England he insisted on returning to the trenches in December 1916. Killed 9th April 1917.

WILLIAM WATSON, SIR, 1858-1935.

Prolific and popular poet, knighted for his patriotism in verse.

ARTHUR GRAEME WEST, 1891-1917.

Educated at Blundell's and Oxford. Volunteered in February 1915. He grew to hate the war, and lost his faith in God. He was convinced he should protest or desert but could not find the courage to do so. He was killed on 3rd April, 1917 at Bapaume.

SOME USEFUL BOOKS RELATING TO THE FIRST WORLD WAR AND ITS POETRY

INDIVIDUAL POETS

Selected Poems of Henry Newbolt, Edited by Patric Dickinson. Hodder & Stoughton, 1981.

Wilfred Owen, War Poems and Others, Edited by Dominic Hibberd. Chatto & Windus, 1973.

The Poems of Wilfred Owen, Edited by Jon Stallworthy. The Hogarth Press, 1985.

Collected Works of Isaac Rosenberg, Edited by Ian Parsons. Chatto & Windus, 1984.

The War Poems, Siegfried Sassoon, Edited by Rupert Hart-Davies. Faber & Faber, 1983.

The Collected Poems of Charles Hamilton Sorley, Edited by Jean Moorcroft Wilson. Cecil Woolf, 1985.

The Works of Edward Thomas, Wordsworth, 1994.

BIOGRAPHIES, COLLECTED LETTERS, AND DIARIES.

Testament of Youth, Vera Brittain. Victor Gollancz, 1933. Virago, 1978.

Vera Brittain, a Life, Paul Berry and Mark Bostridge. Chatto and Windus, 1995.

Rupert Brooke, His Life and Legend, John Lehmann. Weidenfeld & Nicholson, 1980.

Rupert Brooke, The Splendour and the Pain, John Frayn Turner. Breese Books, 1992.

Goodbye to All That, Robert Graves. Penguin, 1960.

Wilfred Owen, Selected Letters, Edited by John Bell. Oxford, 1985.

Wilfred Owen, Jon Stallworthy. Oxford, 1974.

Diaries 1915 - 1918, Siegfried Sassoon, Edited by Rupert Hart-Davis. Faber & Faber, 1983.

Edward Thomas, A Critical Biography, William Cook. Faber & Faber, 1970.

Edward Thomas, the Last Four Years, Eleanor Farjeon. Sutton, 1998.

Under Storm's Wing, Helen Thomas. Carcanet, 1997. All that she wrote about Edward Thomas.

HISTORIES

Britain and the Great War, 1914-1918, J M Bourne. Edward Arnold, 1989.

Blighty, British Society in the Era of the Great War, Gerard DeGroot. Addison Wesley Longman, 1996.

First World War, Martin Gilbert. Weidenfeld & Nicholson, 1994. – Comprehensive, balanced, compassionate, full of fascinating detail, clear and very readable.

Keep the Home Fires Burning, Propaganda in the First World War, Cate Haste. Allen Lane, 1977.

1914-1918, Voices and Images of the Great War, Lyn Macdonald. Michael Joseph, 1988.

The Roses of No Man's Land, Lyn Macdonald. Michael Joseph, 1980.

The Deluge, British Society and the First World War, Arthur Marwick. Open University Press, Macmillan, 1965.

First World War, A J P Taylor. Penguin, 1963. The best short introduction to the war.

The Experience of World War I, J M Winter. Macmillan, 1988. Good text, excellent illustrations.

CLASSIC FICTION OF THE WAR

All Quiet on the Western Front, Erich Remarque. Translated by A W Wheen. Putnam, 1929. Pan/Picador, 1990.

Journey's End, (Stage play) R C Sherriff. Heinemann, 1929, 1993.

LITERARY CRITICISM

Heroes' Twilight: A Study of the Literature of the Great War, Bernard Bergonzi. Constable, 1965. Carcanet, 1996.

The Great War and Modern Memory, Paul Fussell. Oxford, 1975.

Poetry of the First World War, a Selection of Critical Essays, Edited by Dominic Hibberd. Macmillan, 1981.

Out of Battle, the Poetry of the Great War, Jon Silkin. Oxford, 1978.

CONFLICT RESOLUTION TODAY

The Peacemakers - Peaceful Resolution of Disputes Since 1945, Hugh Miall. Macmillan, 1992.

How Wars End, Sydney Bailey. Oxford Clarendon, 1982

INDEX - INCLUDING TITLES OF POEMS

Entries in capitals are titles of poems

POEMS LISTED IN AUTHOR ORDER

Page numbers of poems may be found in the main index

On Receiving News of War
Returning, We Hear the Larks

Siegfried Sassoon

Absolution
Attack
Banishment
Base Details
Counter-Attack
Does it Matter?
Everyone Sang
Fight to a Finish
The General
Glory of Women
Great Men
The Hero
In the Church of St Ouen
I Stood With the Dead
Memorial Tablet
A Mystic as Soldier
Night Attack
On Passing the New Menin Gate
Peace
The Poet as Hero
Prelude: The Troops
The Rear-Guard
Reconciliation
Remorse
Suicide in the Trenches
To Any Dead Officer
Vicarious Christ

Alan Seeger

Rendezvous

Charles Sorley

All the Hills and Vales
From A Call to Action
A Hundred Thousand Million Mites
From The Massacre
Such is Death

To Germany
When You See Millions of the
Mouthless Dead

Lesbia Thanet

In Time of War

Edward Thomas

And You, Helen
As the Teams Head-Brass
The Cherry Trees
For These
In Memoriam
Lights Out
Melancholy
No One Cares Less Than I
No One so Much as You
Out in the Dark
Rain
This is no Case of Petty Right or
Wrong
The Trumpet

Walter Turner

Death's Men

Katherine Tynan

Joining the Colours

R E Vernède

A Listening Post

William Watson

To the Troubler of the World
Veritas Victrix

Arthur Graeme West

God, How I Hate You
Night Patrol

Some useful organisations relevant to students of war poetry and war and peace studies

Poetry

The Poetry Library, Royal Festival Hall, Level 5, London SE1 8XX.
Phone, 0170 921 0943. Information service and loans. Open Tuesday to Sunday, 11 am to 8 pm.

The Poetry Society, 22 Betterton Street, London WC2H 9BU Phone 0171 240 4810.

Birmingham Library Services, Central Library, Chamberlain Square, Birmingham B3 3HQ. Phone 0121 235 2615. Research collection of war poetry.

The Wilfred Owen Association, 17 Belmont, Shrewsbury, Shropshire SY1 1TE   Phone, 01743 235904.

Edward Thomas Fellowship, Butler's Cottage, Halswell House, Goathurst, Bridgwater, Somerset TA5 2DH.

War and peace studies

Imperial War Museum, Lambeth Road, London SE1 6HZ. Phone, 0171 416 5000.

Ministry of Defence, Main Building, Horseguards Avenue, London SW1A 2HB Phone, 0170 218 9000.

NATO (North Atlantic Treaty Organisation), 1110, Brussels, Belgium.   Phone, (2) 728-41-11.

Campaign Against the Arms Trade (CAAT), 11 Goodwin street, London N4 3HQ   Phone, 0171 281- 0297.

United Nations Association of Great Britain and Northern Ireland (UNA), 3 Whitehall Court, London SW1A 2EL   Phone, 0170 930 2931.

Peace Pledge Union, 41b Brecknock Road, London N7 0BT   Phone, 0171 424 9444.

Royal Institute of International Affairs, 10 St James's Square, London SW1Y 4LE Phone 0171 957 5700.

University of Bradford School of Peace Studies, Richmond Road, Bradford BD7 1DP   Phone 01274 232323.

University of Lancaster Richardson Institute (Dept of Politics and International Relations), Cartmel College, Lancaster LA1 4YL   Phone 01524 65201

Mediation UK, Telephone Avenue, Bristol BS1 4BS   Phone 0117 904 6661

Also published by Saxon Books

MINDS AT WAR
The Poetry and Experience of the First World War

The largest anthology of First World War Poetry available – 250 poems by 80 poets, concentrating on the great classic poems of the war (Sassoon, Owen, Graves, and others). Also includes poetry written as propaganda, poetry written by women, and popular verse. A substantial historical background traces the development of propaganda, opinion, and personal responses to war from the pre-war period to the Treaty of Versailles. Text is supported with extracts from speeches and writings by politicians, pundits, the press, poets' diaries, letters and autobiographies. Illustrated with photographs, maps, and drawings.

410 pages PB ISBN 0 952 8969 0 7   £13-99